Inside Ballet Technique

Inside
Ballet Technique

**Separating Anatomical Fact
from Fiction
in the Ballet Class**

Illustrations by Naomi Rosenblatt

Valerie Grieg

**A Dance Horizons Book
Princeton Book Company, Publishers**

A Dance Horizons Book
Princeton Book Company, Publishers
PO Box 831
Hightstown, NJ 08520

Cover design by Frank Bridges
Interior design by Elizabeth Anne O'Donnell
Cover photography by David Cooper of ballerina Evelyn Hart

Library of Congress Cataloging-in-Publication Data
Grieg, Valerie.
    Inside ballet technique : separating anatomical facts from fiction in the
ballet class / Valerie Grieg.
        p.   cm.
    "A Dance Horizons book."
    ISBN 978-0-87127-191-4
    1. Ballet dancing.   I. Title.
GV1788.G79   1994
792.8—dc20   93-4804

Printed in Canada

For Juli

Contents

The Weight-bearing Foot
The Foot and the Turnout
Pointe Work
Muscles of the Lower Leg and Foot
Questions for You to Answer

Acknowledgments

This book owes its being to two remarkable women—Juli Nunlist, who taught me how to write, and Irene Dowd, who taught me how the body works. My early attempts to integrate these new disciplines with my own expertise in ballet technique were clumsy, to put it mildly. Yet never by the twitch of a lip or the flicker of an eyebrow did either of these two mentors betray their awareness of my inadequacies. My gratitude to and affection for both is unbounded.

As time went on (and much time went on), many others contributed to the enterprise—too many to name. Colleagues, students, dancers, doctors and physical therapists read the text and made suggestions, with no thought of thanks but with genuine belief in the need for a book such as this, written expressly for ballet dancers. To them, we are all indebted—author and readers alike. But special thanks are due to a few special people:

Stephanie Woodard, whose extensive experience in the fields of both dance and writing was always generously at my disposal. Her assistance in preparing this manuscript has been invaluable.

Marilyn Klaus, who willingly offered her sensitive dancer's body and fine dancer's mind for any experiment I might devise to try out a new insight or to search for the grain of truth in the latest New York fad.

My friend and former colleague Janet Karin, some of whose words must inevitably appear in this text, for a lifetime's exchange of ideas and discoveries.

And last, but so very far from least, grateful thanks to Dorris and Catherine Carlson, under whose hospitable roof this work was conceived, discussed, revised, discussed, duplicated, discussed, and eventually finished.

Introduction

We learn to dance by dancing. There can be no substitute for the experience of moving a finely tuned instrument through space, with mind and body in subtle harmony. "Just do, dear," Balanchine was said to have exhorted his dancers, and dancers everywhere took his point.

Yet today's dancer is in a problematical position. Rather than being carefully nurtured by teachers who are all schooled in the same tradition (as is the case in the state-supported ballet institutions around the world), most pre-professional students are exposed to many different mentors, who are likely to have varying backgrounds and opinions. In technique classes, conflicting explanations are routinely offered for the most basic of precepts: Use of buttocks? How much turnout? To force or not to force? Which muscles? Pull up what? High chests? Locked knees? Square hips? Sometimes "just doing" presents more difficulties than anyone might reasonably expect.

Controversy is, of course, the lifeblood of any art form, and the training of dancers is no stranger to it. Dynamics, rhythm, motivation, phrasing and flow are subject to scrutiny every time a dancer moves, and all are subject to varying opinions of teachers — opinions based on their own experience as dancers. And this is as it should be. But many of the questions bothering our young dancers and, in some cases, their teachers, are about *fundamental body mechanics.* These are scientific realities and should not be presented as matters of opinion.

Teachers, too, are in an unenviable position in this regard. There is no paucity of information out there. Physical educators have pioneered and thoroughly developed the study of mechanics and anatomy in relation to human movement; the result is the recognized science of kinesiology, now taught in many universities. Dance is the natural beneficiary of this work. There is also an abundance of information on this subject in the form of books, films, videos and magazine articles. The problem, however, from the point of view of both the dancer and teacher, is two fold: the scientific vocabulary is often intimidating and much of the information seems to us to be irrelevant to the technique of classical ballet, sometimes running counter to our own knowledge and experience.

Busy teachers have neither the time nor the patience to figure out, much less to remember, that "anterior superior iliac spine" is the anatomical term for the hip bones. And dancers simply do not care that the gluteals are the muscles that are activated when they are climbing stairs or that the adductors are the principal muscles used in horseback riding —why should they? The debate about the role of these two muscle groups in the turnout of the thighs, on the other hand, is of vital interest.

Most anatomists, kinesiologists, and other movement specialists have no more than a rudimentary knowledge of ballet technique. Again, we can ask: why should they? Their concern has been with movement in general; if dance has played any part in their lives it is likely to have been modern dance. Almost invariably, they fail to take into account the process of natural selection that takes place as ballet students move on to a higher level — a process effectively eliminating the more obviously unsuited. Our experts are apt to view the more advanced aspects of technique with alarm: a full turnout is considered to be a false goal for everyone, a backbend a lethal maneuver, and the whole enterprise a highly dangerous undertaking. Yet classical ballet technique, properly used, conforms to all the natural laws governing human movement and body mechanics.

The aim of *Inside Ballet Technique* is to explore those natural laws and to relate them directly to our ordinary daily classroom pursuit of strength, flexibility, mobility and control. And specifically, to shed some light on those pesky gray areas that seem to crop up again and again, just when we think the issues have been settled.

The book draws heavily on the sciences of anatomy and kinesiology, but the material has been deliberately limited to those fundamentals affecting the everyday execution of the ballet class. Except in passing, the reader will not find any discussion of injuries, difficult bodies, remedial exercises and the like, all of which have been thoroughly covered in other writings.[1] The information is intended mainly to help serious students who have their eye on a professional career, and should be especially useful to those people in transition — the pre-professional student who may have flown the hometown nest; the beginning professional coping with that first year or so of a performing career; the dancer making a career change into teaching.

The Latin names that have been included with the common names throughout the book are meant to give readers, should they so wish, a key to scientific texts. Without these names, it is not even possible to look up an item in the index of an anatomy book. Feel free to ignore them—the text will still be clearly understandable—unless, by chance, you are about to embark on a university dance major, when some familiarity with these terms will get you off to a good start in those science-based courses. The terms "student," "dancer" and "teacher" are used more or less interchangeably throughout the text, as most readers of this book will have been, or probably will be, any one of the three at different stages of their careers.

At the end of each chapter you will find a short list of questions. They are of significant interest to dancers, but there are no answers hidden away in another section of the book. The answers are all in the text, which is easy and, I trust, rewarding to read.

Proficient technique is an essential element in the skill of the dancer, and a clear understanding of how the body functions is bound to make its acquisition easier. It is specifically to that aspect of our many-sided art that the following pages are addressed.

1

Getting It All Straight

This introductory chapter takes a brief look at some of the basic facts about the way the body works; later chapters will examine these facts more closely, applying them to the way we dance.

The Moving Body

The *bones* and *joints* making up the framework of the body are a passive structure, which cannot move by itself. It is the *musculature* that manipulates and controls the skeleton, and so produces movement. The musculature, in turn, is directed by the *nervous system*.

A *joint* is where one bone meets another, and this is where movement takes place. There are several kinds of joints in the body, but the ones of most interest to the dancer are the *freely movable joints*. In these, the bones do not really join, but are held together inside a capsule called, appropriately enough, the *joint capsule*.

Inside the joint capsule there is *cartilage*, which surrounds the bone and acts as a cushion, and *synovial fluid*, which lubricates the whole apparatus.

Stabilizing the Structure

The tough fibrous substance of the joint capsule is formed of *ligament*. Other bands of ligament are attached to the bones outside the joint capsule, crossing it at various angles like cleverly arranged bandages. The function of ligaments is to brace the bones and thus to maintain the stability of the bone structure. So it stands to reason that ligaments, though pliable, are comparatively inelastic and not easily stretched. Once stretched—and this is only possible over a long period— ligaments cannot return to their original length.

1

"Double-jointed" people have overlong ligaments, a condition known as ligamentous laxity. A considerable degree of this condition can signify weakness and lack of stability at the joints and is not, strictly speaking, a good portent for serious dance training. Moderately overlong ligaments, on the other hand, are advantageous to the female dancer, in whom heightened flexibility is a priority. In either case, the degree to which the supporting musculature can be strengthened will determine the amount of control that can eventually be attained.

A torn ligament is said to be *sprained*. Although the injury may seem to heal in a few weeks, the joint will remain vulnerable for about a year, and the dancer would be well advised to be protective of it during that period.

The Role of Muscles

The primary function of *muscles* is to move bones. A typical skeletal muscle has a "belly" that tapers off at each end into a tendon; each tendon is attached to a bone. The muscle belly contracts, and the tendon pulls the bones. Since every muscle crosses at least one joint, the contraction causes movement to be produced. Muscles also function to maintain static positions and they act to resist the force of gravity. Muscles do stretch, but the dancer has to keep working at it: they return to their original length very quickly. A torn muscle is said to be *strained*. Provided the injury is treated with proper respect[2], the muscle, once healed, should not cause any further trouble to the dancer.

A Portrait in Fascia

Surrounding every segment of the body is *connective tissue,* or *fascia.* Its function is to keep every substance in the body separated yet connected. Fascia covers every group of muscles, every nerve, blood vessel, bone and ligament. If you were to remove everything from the body except this strong, resilient tissue, you would have an exact picture, drawn in fascia, of the entire structure. Fascia is made up of elastic fibers and collagen fibers. Collagen fibers are like gelatin; they flow when warm, contributing a good deal to the efficacy of the dancer's warm-up. Elastic fibers will stretch along with muscles and can be torn; "sore muscles" are often little tears in this tissue.

Ligaments, muscles, tendons, cartilage, fascia — everything, in fact, except bones — are often referred to collectively as the *soft tissues.*

A Personal Computer

The *nervous system* directs and controls all movement by and within the body. It consists of the brain and the spinal cord, known as the *central nervous system,* and the nerve fibers that run from the spinal cord to every part of the body and are known as the *peripheral nervous system.* The nervous system has been likened to an extremely efficient computer that provides instant communication between different parts of the body. The dancer determines the action to be performed; the central nervous system immediately programs a complicated sequence of events to accomplish the task.

This brief account serves as an introduction to the nerve-muscle-bone complex, which is directly responsible for bodily motion. Later chapters will examine each of these elements more closely.

A Different Language

Dancers have their own language for movement, and this is the vocabulary used in this book. Occasionally, some anatomical terms are necessary and are listed here for easy reference. You do not need to memorize these terms; they are used sparingly throughout the text.

Directions in Space
Anterior   = toward the front
Posterior = toward the back
Lateral   = away from the
              middle, toward
              the outside
Medial   = toward the middle,
              toward the inside

Directions of Movement
Flexion   = bending
Extension = stretching
Rotation   = the pivoting of a
               bone on its axis
Abduction = moving away from
               the midline of
               the body
Adduction = moving toward the
               midline of the body

Generally speaking, the anatomist uses the expression flexed or flexion in much the same way as a dancer does, but extension is another matter. To the anatomist, a limb is extended when there is no bend at a joint, so that, for instance, the hip joint is extended when it is in a neutral position, such as in standing. When a body part is extended beyond a normal degree (as is the spine in a backbend), it is said to be hyperextended. In a battement to the side, the leg is abducted as it opens and adducted as it closes.

In ballet terminology, the dancer standing on one leg with the other raised high in second position is said to have a good extension. In anatomical terms, there is excellent flexion at the hip joint.

Now it is time to get back to our own language and to an exploration of the way the body functions in classical ballet technique.

2

What We Need to Know About Muscles

Dancers have an intense preoccupation with muscles; most dancers equate a study of the moving body solely with a study of the way in which muscles function. This is not altogether surprising, as it is these hard-working laborers that, physically speaking, are responsible for most of our minor agonies and frustrations. They also make possible most of our major technical accomplishments.

We take the miracle of movement for granted; few of us are curious enough to question its source. But when we do, we discover that movement is initiated not in our muscles, bones, or ligaments, but in that part of the brain known as the cerebral cortex.

Muscles and the Nervous System

We unconsciously visualize the movement we wish to perform, and the central nervous system obliges us by setting in motion the necessary chain of events to accomplish the undertaking. The various muscle groups are automatically programmed; they have no need for decisions on our part. We do not give our muscles any instructions when we run to catch a bus.

In their research, kinesiologists have shown us that it is the *shape* of the designated movement pictured in the cerebral cortex, as well as the *goal*—"the desire to do," as Mabel E. Todd has written in *The Thinking Body*—that triggers the movement response. This information is of particular interest to dancers, as no other physical activity concerns itself so much with shapes or is more intensely goal-oriented. To quote again from Todd, "What actually happens is that we get a picture from the teacher's words or his movements, and the appropriate action takes place within our own bodies to reproduce this picture." She goes on to point out that "the result is successful in proportion to our power of interpretation and amount of experience."

Success also depends on keeping the intricate and precise balance of the two systems, nervous and muscular, in good working order. When you consider that the nervous system is also the seat of all creative, emotional, and intellectual undertakings, you may conclude that we owe it a great deal more awareness than we customarily give it.

The role of the nervous system in movement is a complex one that we only partially understand. We shall return to it and to its effect on the muscular system after a review of the muscles themselves.

The Structure of a Muscle

The muscles that produce movement in our bodies are known as *voluntary,* or *skeletal,* muscles. Arranged in layers, they are described as either "superficial" or "deep." The superficial muscles form the layers that lie nearest to the skin; the deep muscles lie in several layers beneath them.

The body of a muscle consists of hundreds of fibers, each encased in a sheath of very elastic connective tissue, or fascia, and gathered together in bundles. These bundles, in turn, are wrapped in a further envelope of fascia that turns into tendon at the end of the muscle. Tendons are like cords of different lengths and thicknesses; they are extremely strong and not very elastic. The body of the muscle, on the other hand, has a high degree of elasticity. It is attached to bone at either end by tendon, or at one end by tendon and the other by the tissue of the muscle belly itself.

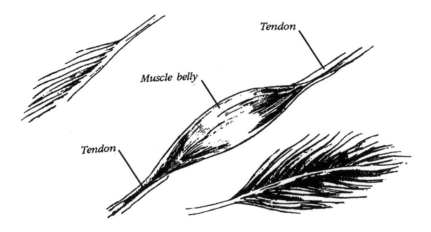

Figure 1. Some predominant shapes of muscles

A muscle can stretch to one-and-a-half times its resting length; of more immediate consequence is its ability to shorten. The muscle body is able to contract to almost half its resting length, pulling the bones at each end. Since every skeletal muscle crosses at least one joint, the contraction causes the bones to move.

The Way Muscles Function

Muscles work in groups, never alone. Every time we make a movement there are two groups of muscles acting simultaneously on the joint. The first group consists of a principal muscle, known as the prime mover, and a number of assistants. This group is known as the *agonists,* after the Greek *agonistes* (competitor, or one who is engaged in a struggle). Placed on the opposite side of the bone is a second group of muscles known as the *antagonists.* To allow movement to happen, the antagonists lengthen when the agonists, or prime movers, contract. The assistants in the agonist group help to produce or control the movement by adding their power to that of the prime mover, or by holding one bone still while another is moved.

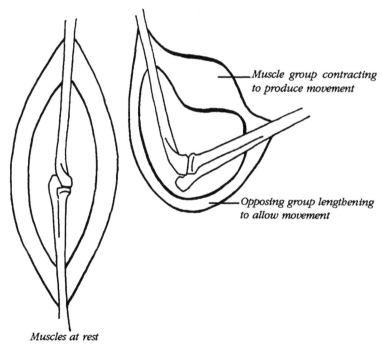

Muscle group contracting to produce movement

Opposing group lengthening to allow movement

Muscles at rest

Figure 2A. Diagram of muscle function

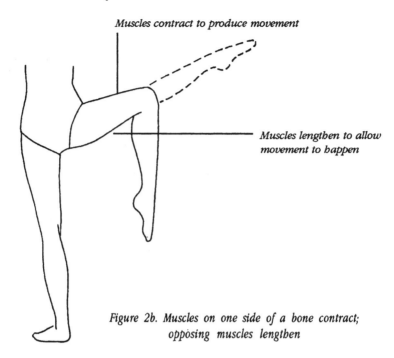

Muscles contract to produce movement

Muscles lengthen to allow movement to happen

Figure 2b. Muscles on one side of a bone contract; opposing muscles lengthen

The same muscle group can act in different capacities, depending on the movement. In a battement to the front, for instance, the muscles in the front of the leg are the prime movers; in a battement to the back they act as antagonists.

A muscle group has three tasks: producing movement, stabilizing, and braking — and it uses a different kind of contraction for each. You have just been introduced to one kind: *concentric* contraction, when the muscle shortens as it contracts, so producing movement. When the muscles act as stabilizers, assisting the ligaments to maintain a given position of the body, they are in *isometric* contraction. In isometric contraction the muscles neither shorten nor lengthen. *Eccentric* contraction is rather more complicated. It occurs as a muscle group provides a braking action against gravity. Although the muscle is lengthening in its capacity as antagonist, some elements of it contract to exert the force needed to control the descent of the limb or body part and prevent it from simply falling down. The moving dancer constantly employs all three types of muscle action.

As the leg unfolds in a développé, for instance, the prime movers shorten, or contract concentrically, while the antagonists lengthen and the stabilizers control the supporting side of the body. Once the position has been reached and is being held, all muscles are in isometric contraction. Then, as the working leg is lowered, those same muscles that caused it to rise will contract eccentrically to prevent the leg from dropping to the floor. The slower the movement, the more force the braking muscles must exert.

But what if our dancer who has completed the développé wishes to lower the working leg swiftly and with force — perhaps to swish it from front to back? The braking action is no longer needed; on the contrary, now gravity must be given some assistance. The muscles initially acting as antagonists now act as prime movers, contracting concentrically to aid gravity in the action.

It follows that in determining the action of a muscle group or in figuring out which muscles are producing a certain movement, we need to have an accurate knowledge of their points of attachment to the bone.

Later chapters of this book contain more information about the actions of specific muscle groups; at this point it is more important to understand the principles involved.

Muscle Tone and Balance

A muscle in its resting state should be alert and ready for action, in a condition known as good muscle tone. Muscles in good tone respond instantly to a stimulus from the central nervous system and also play an important part in effortlessly maintaining our posture. You cannot exercise any conscious control over your muscle tone; its reflex tonus comes from the nervous system. Poor health, fatigue, and depression cause muscle tone to deteriorate, and this shows up in your dancing.

Alertness in muscles must not be confused with tension. A tense muscle is one that is contracted beyond its practical need, and inappropriate tension in the muscles causes many problems. For example, a muscle group that is already partially contracted cannot exert full power when called upon to do its job. The dancer must expend correspondingly more effort to produce the movement. Further, a muscle held in prolonged unremitting contraction will accumulate lactic acid in its fibers. Lactic acid is a waste product of muscle activity that normally dissipates as the activity ceases. An accumulation of this substance can chemically injure the muscle tissue, making it unresponsive to normal stimulus from the nervous system. Too much muscle contraction, especially isometric contraction (gripping the bones in order to stabilize the body), can be as unprofitable as too little.

In movement, muscles will ordinarily alternate between tension and relaxation; in this respect, the rhythm and dynamics of the ballet class are of great importance and spring out of the teacher's own experience as a dancer.

The all-too-rare dancer who moves with the fluid grace of a cat has a perfect balance between the agonists and their antagonists. Much of this blessed state of affairs is related to the nature of the individual's bone structure and central nervous system, but the equilibrium can be damaged by strengthening one muscle group at the expense of its opposite, or by cultivating flexibility at the expense of strength. By the same token, the less endowed dancer can achieve a good measure of balance by working correctly under a knowledgeable teacher, as the classical ballet class in its traditional form has just such a muscular logic built in. As extra insurance, however, it makes good sense for an ambitious dancer to undertake a supplementary conditioning program to ensure optimal muscle balance. Andrea Watkins and Priscilla Clarkson, in *Dancing Longer, Dancing Stronger,* describe an excellent program.

A Word About Stretching

In dance studios throughout the world, when dancers are not actually in motion, they will be found stretching. The type of stretching most commonly undertaken is that of "checking into the body" — determining today's range of motion, easing out little tender spots, mobilizing the body for action or keeping it mobilized for further action. Although many teachers of the old school remain firm in their belief that no stretching whatever should take place until after the barre, there is no problem with this type of stretching. It is one of the dancer's most useful tools and a way of giving the body some much deserved care and attention.

Figure 3. Checking into the body

Forceful stretching of the muscles to increase the range of motion is a different matter. It is important to remember that overall flexibility is dictated by bone structure and the length of the ligaments supporting that structure. Improve your body alignment; this will help to stretch out your ligaments and relax your muscles, and should eventually heighten flexibility. But since there will always be a few areas of muscular tightness to be dealt with from time to time, you need to be acquainted with a phenomenon known as the *stretch reflex.*

In simple terms, a stretched muscle behaves as a piece of elastic does: when let go, it springs back into place. It is useless to attack the muscle with

Figure 4. Increasing the range of motion

short, sharp pulls — bouncing, though pleasurable, is ineffective and often counterproductive, as the muscle may tighten in reaction. To attain your goal of lengthening the muscle, you need, first of all, a thoroughly warmed-up body and a degree of calm concentration. Then you need to move slowly and gently into the stretch and *stay in it* for as long as possible. The muscle and its antagonists will go through several stages of activity, finally inhibiting the reflex. The approximate

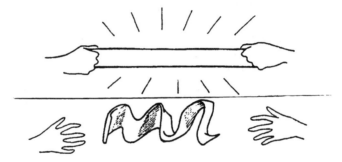

Figure 5. The action of the stretch reflex

length of time the stretch should be sustained seems to be a matter of dispute among kinesiologists. Many advise at least ninety seconds or longer; Sally Fitt, writing in *Dance Kinesiology,* recommends a minimum of thirty seconds. I believe that dancers should rely on their own feeling of the muscle releasing, and that a student who has not reached such a degree of awareness should not be performing an unsupervised stretch of this kind.

It is, of course, the antagonists that are being stretched. If they are tight, they will prevent the prime mover from achieving its goal. For instance, to improve your turnout, you do not stretch the muscles responsible for turning out the thigh; instead, you stretch their antagonists. To use a more specific example, dancers know that tight hamstring muscles at the back of the knee will prevent the knee from fully stretching in a développé. Contrary to a belief widely held among students, however, it is not the hamstrings that act on the knee to stretch it, but rather the large quadriceps muscle on the front of the thigh.

This thought leads us to a very real dilemma in the teaching of ballet technique. Such is the power of the mind that repeated emphasis on the action of certain susceptible muscles can produce bulk. In discussing muscle action in the classroom, most experienced teachers would prefer to speak of the antagonist — the muscle that is lengthening —rather than of the one that is contracting to produce the movement. These tactics often lead to misconceptions, as in the quad-hamstring confusion just mentioned. Teachers must solve these matters in their own way, but an occasional mention of the fact that the lengthening muscle is *allowing* movement, not producing it, would be helpful, especially to the less advanced student.

Each individual muscle fiber is capable of either full contraction or none at all. The fibers work in relays, however, so that the degree of contraction in the muscle body as a whole can be exactly suited to the task it has to perform. When a muscle is contracted lightly, some of its fibers are operating while the rest remain inactive.

This delicate programming can be upset when dancers are consciously "using" a muscle. One of the most endearing qualities that all dancers share is the tendency to overdo, and this trait is never more apparent than in their attitude toward their muscles. We feel strong sensations in our muscles only when they are operating at full capacity, but it would be well to remember that we do not need a bulldozer to move a pile of leaves.

Imagery — the Dancer's Magic Tool

The preceding discussion does not mean, of course, that there should never be a reference to muscles in a ballet class, or that a knowledge of muscles and the way they function is of only marginal value to the dancer. Apart from all other considerations, there is the constant struggle we undertake with those recalcitrant muscles that are *preventing* a movement we are set on doing. But the practice of pinpointing the muscles that must be "used" to *produce* a movement raises a question or two.

We are all familiar with at least one dancer who is "seized up" —who seems unable to make a fluid movement, or even a natural one. For one reason or another, there has been some interference in the normal connections between nervous, muscular and skeletal systems. There are those of us who believe that this unhappy condition can sometimes be caused by the obsessive emphasis that some dancers place on the role of muscle contraction in the execution of movement.

A more effective way of working is to use a knowledge of mechanics to devise images designed to feed the central nervous system. The nervous system can then be relied on to choose the right coordination of muscles for the performance of the movement. Up to a point, teachers have always used imagery as a teaching tool, but more often than not the images have been poetic metaphors and flights of fancy which may, or may not, have influenced our dancing or helped to solve a particular movement problem. "Imagine you are walking on a cloud, darling," is one I remember from my own dancing days. The resulting reluctance to place my weight firmly on my feet caused me to give an impression of walking on a field of tacks.

These days, the practice of visualization has developed into a genuine technique, with scientifically based images that yield much more predictable results. The ball started rolling with Mabel E. Todd, who combines science with poetry in her books *The Hidden You* and *The Thinking Body*; it was picked up by her disciple Dr. Lulu Sweigard, who developed out of imagined movement a teaching method that she called *ideokinesis*. Her book, *Human Movement Potential*, contains insights that are of great benefit to dancers. Since then, research conducted by other physical educators, especially in the field of sports training, has resulted in the use of imagery snowballing into an invaluable instrument with which to refine movement.

All dancers have had some experience with the efficacy of visualization. Are there any dancers who have not dreamt of turning countless pirouettes, only to find, next morning in the studio, that their turns are much improved? This experience loses some of its mystery when we understand, however

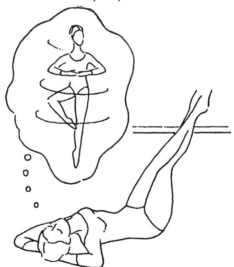

Figure 6. Visualization at work

sketchily, the immense power of the nervous system. Visualizing a specific skill, such as a leap or a turn, will work wonders, assuming (and this is an important aspect of putting specific imagery to use) that you have a clear picture of the shape of the movement and the placement of all body parts. Flash a mental picture of the movement across your mind just before performing it, and the result may surprise you.

Images that send messages to particular parts of the body are not difficult to invent. It is always effective to picture the action of the bones themselves going about their business. For example, when executing an arabesque, visualize the curves and rotations the spine is making as you raise your leg to the back. If the picture is accurate, your line will be beautiful even if your extension is not a spectacular one. Sometimes a picture of an object or a mechanical gadget can be pressed into service. To keep your balance during a pirouette, for instance, imagine a sliding curtain rod running through your central axis, from head to toe. As you turn, see the rod lengthening at each end. This image[3] works for most dancers, but you must be able to see that central axis accurately.

Initially it is the teacher who will suggest the images, and the less advanced student should continue to rely on this source, as hazy and inaccurate visualization can do more harm than good. But the advanced dancer should try to play an active role in the creative process, as not all images are equally effective for all dancers. In addition, images tend to wear out and need to be renewed and refreshed from time to time. Dr. Sweigard puts it this way: "An image used repeatedly tends to lose its value as a challenge to subcortical patterning of muscle coordination." No teacher can be expected to have an inexhaustible supply of fresh images to fit every possible physical and psychological type, and some excellent teachers do not have the knack at all. For the magic to work, and to keep on working, dancers should be prepared to invent some images of their own.

This undertaking presents no problem to the dancer who has a useful knowledge of body mechanics and a good eye for movement. In fact, it is a lot of fun. You will come across many effective images in the following chapters of this book but, even more important, you will be armed with the information you need to conjure up some strictly personal ones.

Questions For You To Answer:

What is the principal task performed by muscles?

There are two other important tasks. Can you name them?

Why are good muscle tone and optimal muscle balance so important to the dancer?

Why is bouncing an ineffective way to stretch muscles?

What makes imagery such an effective tool for the dancer?

3

The Stem of Aplomb

There is hardly a movement in dance in which the spinal column does not play a dominant role, and this truth holds firm for classical ballet technique as much as for any other dance form. Although the limbs initiate movement and give vital support, it is not with our legs or our arms that we balance, turn, change direction or add nuance to our dancing.

"The stem of aplomb is the spine." This observation by the famous Russian pedagogue Agrippina Vaganova is often quoted, but rarely fully explained. Instead, dancers are expected to "get the feeling," advice which, incidentally, is given by Mme. Vaganova herself in her book, *Basic Principles of Classical Ballet*. No one will deny that getting the feeling is the quintessence of all dance technique, especially when it comes to aplomb — or stability — yet muscular sensations alone do not tell us the whole story, and mystical images, as we have already established, may inspire but do not necessarily inform.

Each area of the spine is capable of a specific type of movement and has a normal range of motion. The range increases as training progresses, though only within limits prescribed by the spinal structure. The dancer who understands exactly which sections will bend – which will twist, and why – is one step ahead when it comes to gaining more flexibility and control.

The Spinal Column

In dancing, as in everyday movement, the main function of the spine is to support the weight of the head, rib cage, and shoulder girdle while transferring this weight to the pelvis. Its architecture makes it uniquely suited to this purpose.

There are thirty-three bones, or vertebrae, in the spinal column. Of these, five at the lower end are fused together to form the sacrum, and four are

15

fused to form its appendage, the coccyx, or tailbone. These nine bones are contained within the pelvis and cannot be moved independently. Consequently, some kinesiology texts refer to the spinal column as consisting of twenty-four bones.

The spine has four curves if you look at it from the side. The *cervical* spine is the small curve at the top, made up of seven vertebrae. Starting at the level of the ears are the atlas, the first vertebra, and the axis, the second. The seventh vertebra is more prominent than the rest; you can

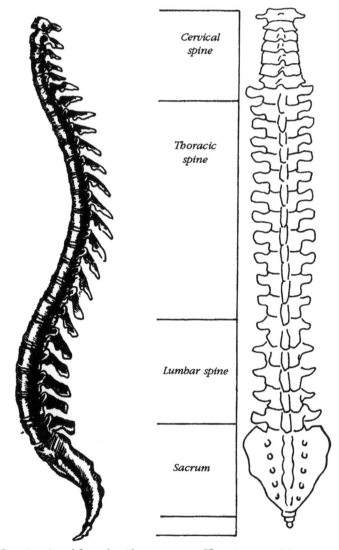

Cervical spine

Thoracic spine

Lumbar spine

Sacrum

The spine viewed from the side   *The spine viewed from the back*

Figure 7. *The spine*

see it and feel it at the base of your neck. Below it and curving the other way are twelve vertebrae that get progressively larger; they form the *thoracic* spine. To these, the ribs are attached. Reversing the curve again are five much larger vertebrae forming the *lumbar* spine: the "hollow" of your back. Last comes the *sacral curve,* comprising the sacrum and coccyx.

Discs of spongy elastic cartilage are sandwiched between the vertebrae;

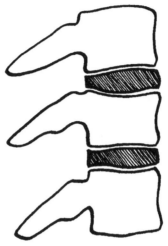

Figure 8. Vertebrae and discs

they prevent friction and act as shock absorbers. The bones and discs are kept in place by strong ligaments running the entire length of the spine. Also running the length of the spine, on either side of it, is a group of very strong muscles, collectively called the erector spinae. As its name implies, the principal task of this muscle group is to hold the spine erect.

The curves of the spine function as additional shock absorbers and are very important to the dancer. The basic stance of classical ballet elongates the spine so that these curves are diminished, though by no means eliminated. Provided the pelvis is not tucked under, a back that appears quite straight from the side view actually does retain its necessary curves. The differences in the size and slant of the bony projections on the back of each vertebra (known as spinous processes) are responsible for this illusion.

The lengthening of the spine has some important results. The diminished curves make for a stronger spine, as it is in the transition areas, where one curve flows into the next, that the spine is most vulnerable to injury. The sharper the curves, the greater the vulnerability. In addition, and of more immediate consequence to the ballet dancer, the center of gravity is raised, making for more speed and mobility, and the lengthened muscles of the

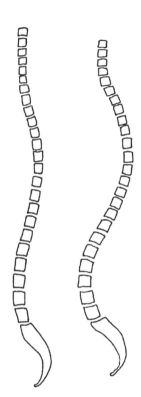

Figure 9. Diagram of dancer's elongated spine and a relaxed spine

back enhance its flexibility. The center of gravity is that midpoint of all body weight, normally found in the pelvic area. A high center of gravity enhances the dancer's quality of lightness and mobility; a low center gives an earthbound impression. The center of gravity is constantly shifting when the dancer is in motion; the moving dancer instinctively manipulates it to maintain control.

You can move your spine by bending, twisting, or shifting it, or by tilting your pelvis. The curves are interdependent — any alteration of one will affect the others. Thus, for instance, a "poked" or forward head is nearly always accompanied by an exaggerated backward curve of the thoracic spine, which in turn will surely affect the lumbar area. Mercifully, the dancer's persistent attention to lengthening throughout the entire spine gradually takes care of most such problems.

Getting Centered

To properly understand the way the spine functions you need to be familiar with the differing shapes of the vertebrae, as it is these that

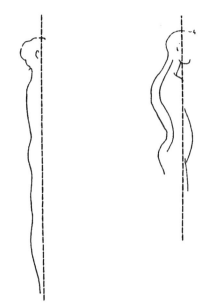

Figure 10. The curves of the spine are interdependent; any deviation of one affects the others

determine the type of movement that is possible in each particular area.

Except for the atlas and the axis, the vertebrae share certain similarities. Figure 11 shows three vertebrae seen from above. Each has a large bony mass known as its *body*; from this mass two projections form a ring through which the spinal cord passes. This ring in turn has three projections: two known as *lateral processes*, which branch to the side, and another, called the *spinous process*, going to the back.

Lateral processes serve as points of attachment for the ribs and for the muscles of the trunk. Spinous processes are the knobs you can feel down the entire length of your back. *One of the misconceptions we must discard is that these knobs are "the spine."* When you are instructed to lengthen the spine, the reference is to the column formed by the *bodies* of the vertebrae, stacked one upon the other and running through the trunk in a much deeper, more central position than we usually imagine. Similarly, the oft-repeated instruction "center your spine" is a reference to the alignment of those same bodies of the vertebrae. The dancer who keeps this fact in mind will no longer be mystified by these directives and will experience not only greater control but also an almost immediate increase in range of movement.

Try, for example, a grand rond de jambe, visualizing the action taking

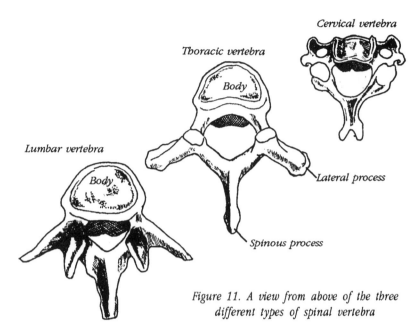

*Figure 11. A view from above of the three
different types of spinal vertebra*

place in that central axis. Or better still, until you have more information about the way extensions of the leg affect movements of the spine, try simply standing on two feet, bending and twisting your trunk in every direction, while concentrating on that column deep within you. You will feel a new freedom of movement. The truly talented dancer always seems to move from this deep-seated place.

Movement Possibilities and Limitations in Each Area

It is the differences in the shape and angle of the spinous processes that play a major role in determining the type and range of movement in each area.

Anatomists use a serviceable system of abbreviations in referring to the individual vertebrae of the spine, which they name (by letter and number) from the top of each area. For example, the seventh cervical vertebra, at the base of the neck, is known as C.7. The bone immediately below, which is the top of the thoracic segment, is known as T.1. This system will serve us admirably in the following pages.

The *cervical spine* is the most mobile of all the spinal areas. These seven bones, which form the neck, have spinous processes that are short and almost horizontal. Their size and angle permit the turning and bending of the head in all directions, movements impeded only by any tightness in the supporting muscles.

Each of the two top vertebrae, the atlas and the axis, has an individual shape. The atlas (so named after the legendary Titan who, as punishment for a revolt against the gods, was obliged to support the heavens with his head) is formed like a ring, without a body and with only rudimentary processes. The skull, which is one of the heaviest bony masses in the body, is supported by this one bone at the top of the spine, in line with the entrance to the ears. The shape of the axis departs from that of the other vertebrae in that its body projects upward to fit into the ring of the atlas, forming a pivot on which the atlas, carrying the head, turns.

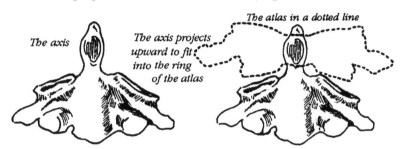

Figure 12. The axis acts as a pivot on which the head turns

Sideways inclination of the head is also initiated here. *In fact, all small movements of the head are initiated in these topmost joints of the neck, between the ears.* These slight inclinations — the nod, the glance, the questioning look, the suggestions of acquiescence, humility, hauteur, and countless other expressions—are the most elegant and gracious movements in dance, and there is no single movement that more quickly repays specific visualization. The image of a skull atop a bone is hardly a poetic one, but the glittering tiara on the crown of the head— an image much favored by teachers of the younger set—will never be worn by a dancer who has not mastered these subtle movements.

Maximum sideways bending of the neck takes place at the seventh cervical vertebra (C.7), a useful fact to point out to beginners, who always seem to have difficulty in isolating this head movement. You can locate this bone by hanging your head forward; it will protrude at the base of your neck.

The vertebrae between the axis and C.7 are the site of maximum forward and backward bending of the entire spine. In a backbend the pull of gravity adds to the already considerable weight of the skull, and the extended spine puts a great strain on the muscles of the neck until these have been developed and strengthened. To avoid the all-too-common error of a "collapsed neck" and the consequent dead weight of the head during the backbend, it is advisable for less advanced dancers always to turn the head during this movement. The strong, thick muscle that can then easily be seen at the side of the neck (sterno-cleido-mastoid) will contract eccentrically to support the head. Students will recognize the sketch as the beginning of the first cambré at the barre, but they are not always aware that the turning of the head has a functional as well as a stylistic purpose.

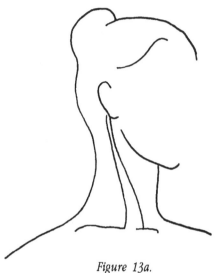

Figure 13a.
An important muscle in the neck

Figure 13b. Support for the head
in a beginning backbend

The balance of the entire body is affected by the carriage of the head. Sensations of motion, weight, and position in space are derived from organs in the inner ear. Awareness of your orientation in space will be impaired if you continually hold your head off center. Also, needless to say, the upper curve is disturbed when the head is askew, which in turn affects all other areas of the spine, setting up muscular strains and tensions throughout the trunk. A poised and centered head is one of the first essentials for good placement. It should feel quite free of the rest of the cervical spine.

The *thoracic spine* is the least mobile segment of the spinal column; its movements are nevertheless the most interesting of all three areas, and heightened flexibility in the region is of primary importance to the dancer.

In Figure 7, it can be seen that the spinous processes increase in size from top to bottom — as does their sharp downward angle—so that they overlap like shingles on a roof.[4] The lateral processes command our attention here, as each has a rib attached to it. These two circumstances combine to make forward and backward bending minimal throughout most of the thoracic spine, although there is less restriction at its base, where the change of direction to the next curve takes place. Here the angle of the spinous processes is not quite so sharp, and two pairs of "floating" ribs allow greatly increased freedom of motion.

It is in sideways bending and rotation (or twisting), however, that the thoracic spine comes into its own. The dancer's back, with its lengthened spine and strong flexible muscles, allows a great deal more rotation than is normal, the rib cage being, of course, a limiting factor. Rotation of the spine occurs in countless movements of classical ballet. It enters into the curves of all the basic body positions, doing double duty in arabesques and attitudes. It gives impetus to turns and facilitates quick changes of direction. As épaulement, it lends distinction and shading to the most basic of movements.

The top three vertebrae of the thoracic spine (above the shoulder blades) have shorter, more horizontal processes than does the rest of the segment; these allow some bending which complements the action of the much more mobile cervical area. The next four vertebrae, T.4-7, are located in the region between the shoulder blades. All motion is diminished and even rotation is minimal. Yet this segment is hardly lifeless; it contributes its share by lengthening dynamically during movement. In a backbend, for instance, or in an arabesque, the curve in this area stretches and flattens, and so assists the more flexible areas to achieve their purpose.

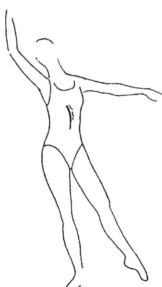

Figure 14. Épaulement initiated in the thoracic spine

Mobility begins to be restored in the area just under the shoulder blades and reaches a peak at T.12 which is just above the hollow of your back. If you curl your spine forward, T.12 will bulge. Maximum rotation takes place here. In this area the spiraling movement of the spine for arabesques and attitudes and all body positions is initiated. Épaulement, while appearing to take place in the shoulders, begins in these lower thoracic vertebrae. It is here that dancers "wind up" their bodies for multiple pirouettes, and here, too, is the region that participates with the lumbar spine in deep backbends and high leg extensions.

Strength and flexibility in the thoracic area of the spine is an essential part of a dancer's technical equipment, and more attention could profitably be paid to it during a student's training. At the lower levels of training, correct placement is the most potent tool in this pursuit; students in higher levels need a greater use of épaulement in the daily class than they usually get.

The *lumbar spine* is the hollow of your back. If you spread your thumbs and place your hands firmly on the top of your pelvis, your thumbs will almost be touching L.4. L.5 is below the surface of the pelvis. Rotation is almost absent in the lumbar spine, but its large vertebrae with their short and sturdy processes lend themselves well to the task of bending.

Backward bending (in anatomical language, hyperextension of the lumbar spine) warrants special consideration because of its role in all backward extensions of the leg. The deep backbends and high sustained arabesques of the female dancer strike fear of injury into the hearts of movement educators, yet it is not practical to restrict the flexibility of a well-trained dancer. Instead, the lumbar spine must be lengthened to eradicate any "collapse" in the lower back during the backbend and to avoid any too sharp angle in the area as the leg is raised to the back. The thoracic spine, its mobility heightened by training, must absorb some of the curve. "Stretch up before you bend back" and "lift out of your waist in arabesque" are two standard commands that produce good results, though dancers would benefit by a more detailed explanation of the reason behind these directives.

Strong abdominal muscles play an important role in the safety of these movements. In the backbend they function in eccentric contraction to resist the pull of gravity and in concentric contraction to assist the return to the upright position; in the arabesque they sustain the lengthened spine and lift the weight of the pelvis off the supporting leg, thus maintaining maximum stretch of the iliopsoas (see page 33).

For our purposes the *sacrum* and the *coccyx* move as one. The sacrum at the base of the spine forms the back of the pelvic girdle; it

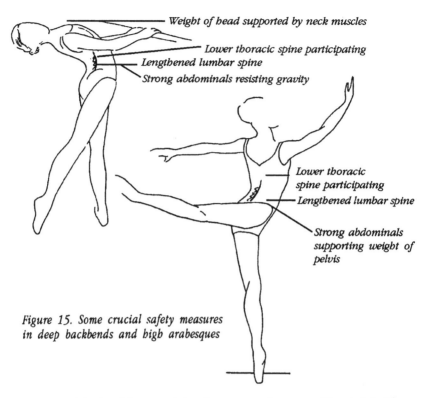

Weight of head supported by neck muscles

Lower thoracic spine participating

Lengthened lumbar spine

Strong abdominals resisting gravity

Lower thoracic spine participating

Lengthened lumbar spine

Strong abdominals supporting weight of pelvis

Figure 15. Some crucial safety measures in deep backbends and high arabesques

connects with the hip at a joint known as the sacroiliac joint. The ligaments binding this joint are so strong that there is virtually no movement of the sacrum that is independent of the pelvis. By the same token, because of this connection, any movement of the pelvis involves the lumbar spine, and in turn is reflected higher up in the spinal column.

I must now remind you that this analytical separation of the spine, area by area and vertebra by vertebra, is useful only for the purpose of studying the way each part contributes to the action of the whole. In reality, the areas flow imperceptibly into one another, and any adjustment of one is immediately reflected in the others; thus it is the spine in its entirety that we must keep in view in considering its action. And nowhere is this consideration more important than in our placement.

The Dancer's Stance

Posture, placement, pull-up...The principles governing a dancer's stance are essentially uncomplicated, yet questions about these matters are always the first to arise in any discussion in the studio. Young dancers are confused by a barrage of instructions, some of them conflicting and most of them unnecessary. Rhonda Ryman, writing in *Dance in Canada,*[5] describes the habitual commands as being "like catechisms of the dance class." The exhortations are likely to commence as soon as the dancers are lined up at the barre. "Flatten your back," "Tighten your buttocks," "Pull up your thighs," "Pull in your stomach," "Pull down your shoulders," "Lift your ribs," "Raise your chest..." By now our dancer is all but immobilized. And no wonder. These are corrections, not basic principles, and should be specific to an individual, not general. Even when specific, their value ranges from the doubtful to the downright harmful, as later chapters of this book will disclose.

In examining these fundamental elements of technique, it may be prudent to define the terms customarily used in the ballet class. *Posture* is the dancer's stance. It is the wellspring from which all movement flows. The moving dancer continually returns to the basic stance, gradually educating the bodily reflexes and establishing the most efficient framework within which to function. *Placement* is the relationship of each part of the body to the next, in positions and in movement, and the resulting distribution of body weight. Though sometimes the two terms are used interchangeably, most often posture refers to a dancer standing at the barre, and placement refers to the same dancer in movement. The basic body positions through which, in traditional ballet technique, all movement passes, must be well placed if the dancer is to maintain control. *Pull-up* is an elongation of the body which raises the center of gravity and increases the dancer's mobility. The key to good

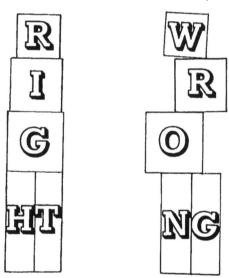

Figure 16. The bony masses of the body are stacked like building blocks

posture is the correct alignment of the spine. The bony masses of the skeleton — head, rib cage, and pelvis — are stacked vertically, like building blocks, over their base, the legs and feet. This balanced position, with the shoulder girdle hanging easily on top of the rib cage, causes the line of gravity — the imaginary vertical line that exactly bisects the weight of the body — to fall through the center of the structure. All parts, on either side of the line, balance each other.

Viewed from the front or the back, the line bisects the body into two symmetrical halves. Viewed from the side when the dancer is standing with parallel feet, the line passes from the top of the head to a point just behind the ear, and on through the centers of the shoulder, rib cage, pelvis and hip joints respectively, to continue down through the knee joint and into the foot, in front of the ankle.

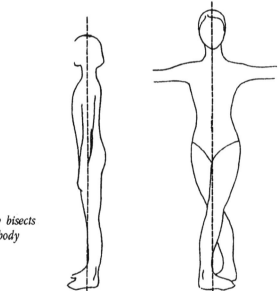

Figure 17.
The line of gravity bisects
the weight of the body

A dancer standing in a properly closed fifth position answers to the above description, except that the turned-out postion causes the view of the lower limbs to be reversed — the side view just described for parallel feet now becomes the back (or front) view.

The weight is distributed on three points of the foot — the heel, and the big and little toes. Here I must depart from the accepted wisdom of the movement educators to point out that the weight is not evenly distributed on these three points; the ballet dancer's stance places slightly more weight on the toes than on the heels. The fully turned-out position of the legs automatically places the weight where it belongs.

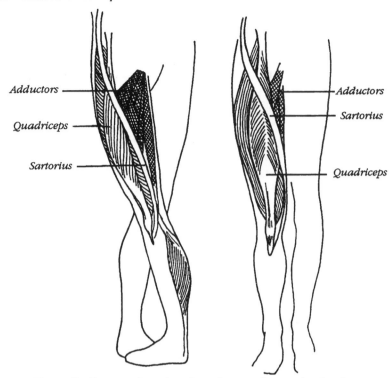

Figure 18. The turned-out leg alters the way the muscles function

Until the turnout is developed, though, attention must be paid to this detail, the importance of which is often overlooked. With the correct slightly forward weight placement, mobility is increased and the hamstrings, the calf muscles, the muscles of the back and the forefoot are all lightly and involuntarily engaged, making a constant contribution to their strengthening process.

The body is now as ideally balanced as possible, with the spine approximately parallel to the line of gravity, so no undue muscular effort should be needed to maintain this upright stance. Important muscles are freed to perform their principal task of moving bones.

It is in the next step that opportunities for error present themselves. All too often young dancers are told to "pull up" without being told *what* to pull up, with distinctly unhappy results. There is no doubt that fads and fancies come and go in the teaching of ballet technique, much as they do in any other field. The instruction "pull up" is of comparatively recent origin—a few decades ago the word was "don't sit on your hips," or "suspend yourself in space." These and other rather vague admonitions, when used in combination by the ever-resourceful dancer, ultimately produced a reasonable facsimile of the desired results. In spite of the tremendous advance in the distribution of information, today's dancer learns by much the same method of trial and error as did the dancer of yesteryear and, having learned, can be just as inarticulate when it comes to passing on the information. Yet there is nothing mysterious or obscure about the pull-up; it is a very simple scientific concept that has always been fundamental to the technique of classical ballet.

The pull-up is a lengthening of the spine from coccyx to atlas. If the action is performed correctly, muscles pulling up the knees and the front of the pelvis (quadriceps and abdominals) are involuntarily engaged. The pelvis must be held in its correct vertical position (see pages 39-41) with the hip crests lifted in front and the sacrum directed firmly downward. There should be no hint of "tucking"—on the contrary, the buttocks are held high on the top of the legs. The spine is then gently lengthened without disturbing the alignment of the body. Imagery works its magic here: "See the spinal column as an ever-expanding silver rod, traveling up to the ceiling and down into the floor." "Pretend you are hanging from the ceiling and your feet are reaching for the floor." "Imagine the base of your spine is an anchor and you have a bunch of balloons tied to the top of your head. Now see the balloons drifting upward and slightly forward."

The opposing forces thus brought to bear on the spinal column by these and other popular images cause the curves to be decreased, elongating the spine and elevating the head. The dancer has grown taller. Gravity, the inherent factor in all human movement, is being more forcefully resisted.

As the student progresses in understanding, special emphasis is placed on lengthening the lumbar spine and here, seemingly, is a paradox: the lumbar spine is lengthened *downward*, not pulled upward. The muscles of the back are extensors of the spine; they *cannot* pull up (see pages 30-31). But the action causes a further diminishing of the spinal curves, so that the dancer has a sense of the *vertebrae* rising upward.

The dancer now feels suspended, poised and ready for action—balanced, but on the edge of the unbalance inherent in all movement. "Pulled up" is not a very apt description of this felicitous state of being, but it seems to be the best we have been able to muster, and it has become part of our ballet language.

Unfortunately, the instruction is frequently misunderstood, resulting in distorted and rigid body positions that fly in the face of common sense. The injunction also seems to have become a catch-all correction for any technical difficulty and is often issued in inappropriate circumstances. The pull-up is an integral part of the way we stand and move, not a trick to be pulled out of the hat momentarily to aid an unstable dancer. Prima ballerina Cynthia Gregory has pointed out that "Balance is *into* the floor. When people tell you to pull up, you're never going to relax."[6]

Returning to the beginning of this section, we are faced with another unhelpful practice—the routine recital of a litany of instructions before the dancer has even begun to move. With separate commands for particular parts of the body and the emphasis on tightening specific muscles, the practice results, at the very least, in disquiet in the minds of students. To be sure, each part of the body has its optimal placement and manner of functioning; the placement of the pelvis, for example, directly affects the placement of all other parts. But the dancer who has a clear idea of the basic concept of alignment for the whole body will have minimal trouble with the parts. And dancers who think mostly in terms of moving bones rather than of contracting particular muscle groups will avoid the ever-present pitfall of excessive rigidity. Rigidly set muscles, especially in the upper body, interfere with our natural postural reflexes. In order to stay balanced and be ready to move, the body constantly makes imperceptible adjustments, departing from and returning to equilibrium. These adjustments are instinctive; all that is required of us is to allow them to happen.

Let no one take this to mean that there is no sensation of muscular activity in maintaining a proper stance. On the contrary, the engagement of all the pertinent muscle groups, especially the abdominals and those of the lower back, can be distinctly felt. But the dancer must learn to tread the fine line between firm control and inappropriate contraction. A dynamic rather than static concept of placement and turnout goes a long way toward achieving this goal.

The experienced teacher will recognize this advice as the proverbial counsel of perfection; the pre-professional dancer has a good deal of tension to work through before reaching an optimal muscular balance. But we must try to banish *unnecessary* tension and give the wisdom of the body a chance to prevail.

Some Postural Muscles of the Trunk

A deep muscle system of the back, the *erector spinae*, is one of the principal sources of the remarkable strength and power of a dancer's back. This system is actually a group of muscles functioning as one; it has been likened to a rope with the various strands intertwining.[7] The erector spinae lies along the spine, on either side of it, and runs from the base of the skull to the sacrum. It assists the ligaments in bracing the spine and holding it erect. It also acts to hyperextend the spine (bend it

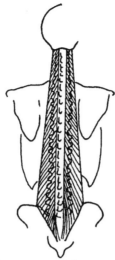

Figure 19. Diagram of the erector spinae

backward) and flex it laterally (bend it to the side). The actions of the erector reinforce those of more superficial muscles, most notably the *latissimus dorsi*, the great muscle of the back, described in Chapter 6. The erector spinae plays a major role in the dancer's habitual lengthening of the spine and, like other muscles of the lower back, it does so by exerting its force downward. As extensors of the spine, these muscles *cannot* pull up. Trying to pull the small of the back up, as we are instructed even by such an eminent authority as V. Kostrovitskaya[8] is like trying to drive a car with the brakes on.

The *abdominal* muscles are divided into two groups, the superficial and deep abdominals. Both groups are important postural muscles; together with the muscles of the hip they establish the position of the pelvis, and they are active in preserving the proper relationship of the pelvis to the rib cage.

The superficial abdominal muscles are the *external* and *internal obliques*, the *transversus abdominis*, and the *rectus abdominis*. Covering the front and sides of the body, they form a corset-like network that is much more extensive than we usually suppose. Did you know, for instance, that those muscles around the waist, on whose strength we rely so much, are abdominals? From high in the ribs—just below the breastbone—down to the groin, and reaching around the sides into the back, they lie in several layers, the deepest being the transverse abdominis, then the obliques, and finally the rectus abdominis, which is the sturdy muscle running on either side of the midline of the body. Study *Figure 20* for a clear picture of the way these muscles are organized.

In movement, the main task of this group of abdominals is that of

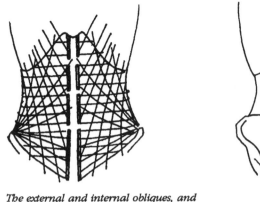
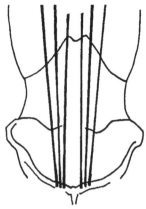

*The external and internal obliques, and
transversus abdominus*

The rectus abdominus

Figure 20. Diagram of the superficial abdominal muscles

flexion—they flex the pelvis on the spine, or the spine on the pelvis. These are the muscles that can be properly described as pulled up, as they shorten to adjust the position of the pelvis. They are the prime movers in bending to either side and in returning to the upright position after a backbend. The abdominals also assist in rotation of the spine; thus the superficial abdominals are active in all movements of the trunk.

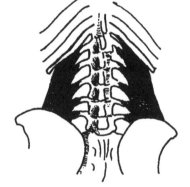

*Figure 21.
The quadratus lumborum*

The deep abdominal muscles are the *quadratus lumborum* and the *iliopsoas.*

The *quadratus lumborum* is a short thick muscle in the posterior abdominal wall, running from the lowest rib to the top of the pelvis and attaching itself to the lumbar vertebrae along the way. This muscle pulls the ribs and the pelvis toward each other, stabilizing the important relationship of these two parts of the body. It also stabilizes the pelvis on the lumbar spine and participates in lateral flexion (sideways bending) of the spine. The length of the quadratus lumborum affects the tilt of the pelvis—a short, tight quadratus lumborum goes hand-in-hand with lordosis (hollow back). The quadratus lumborum is active in any movement that stretches the lumbar spine.

The *iliopsoas* consists of three muscles, the psoas major, the psoas minor and the iliacus. The psoas major is the principal muscle of the group; the psoas minor is relatively unimportant and in some people absent altogether. The psoas major arises at the twelfth thoracic vertebra and also along the lumbar spine and travels diagonally forward and

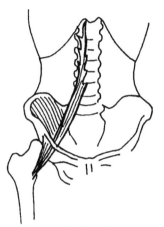

Figure 22. The iliopsoas

downward, crossing the front of the pelvis and joining with the iliacus, whereupon the two muscles then descend (as the iliopsoas) and are inserted into the lesser trochanter of the femur. In this rather surprising manner, the lower spine is attached directly to the femur, or thigh bone, hence its role in the action of the legs.

The iliopsoas (its name usually abbreviated to "psoas" in the dance studio) is a principal flexor of the hip joint. It initiates the bend of the hips in a cambré forward, flexing the spine and the pelvis on the thigh. It is also involved in bending the lumbar spine to the side. In battements and développés, the other thigh flexors initiate the movement, but the iliopsoas quickly assumes the principal role and acts as the sole flexor after the leg has reached 90 degrees. Any malfunctioning of the iliopsoas places a burden on the other thigh flexors, especially the quad.iceps, increasing the work load and thus adding unwanted bulk to the thighs.

This muscle also plays a vital role in the alignment of the legs with the trunk. A tight psoas is accompanied by flexion at the hips and, in a chain reaction, causes disturbance in the placement of the entire body. The resulting hollow back and disengaged hamstrings result in all manner of problems for the dancer, including displacement of the weight behind the line of gravity. Tightness in the psoas also inhibits the raising of the leg in arabesques and attitudes.

Most authorities also credit the iliopsoas with the ability to participate in outward rotation of the thigh, though this opinion has been a matter of dispute. Any advanced-level ballet dancer, however, can attest to the fact that the habitual lengthening of the lumbar spine together with firm control of the muscles of the lower back decidedly increases the ease of turnout. As the psoas is the only muscle of the lower back that connects with the femur, we must give it its due.

This muscle is obviously of crucial importance to the dancer and must be kept in good working order. The most effective way to do this is to pay attention to the placement of the pelvis and to the stretching of the lumbar spine. The customary exercises of classical ballet can be relied upon to strengthen a weak iliopsoas, provided correct placement has been established. A tight iliopsoas can be stretched by any exercise that stretches the area of the groin (the crease where your legs join the trunk).

Other muscles around the area of the hips, especially the gluteals, also participate in establishing our posture. They are described in the following chapter.

Questions For You To Answer:

Can you draw a line representing the curves of the spine?

Where are all small movements of the head initiated?

What are the knobs you can feel down the length of your back?

Which is the least mobile area of the spine? Does it make any contribution to our movement?

What are the benefits resulting from the traditional lengthening of the spine?

Which part of the spine does not bend? Which part does not twist?

4

The Control Center

If the spine is the stem of a dancer's aplomb — or stability — the roots of that stability undoubtedly lie in the pelvis. This beautiful piece of bony architecture is shaped roughly like a bowl, high at the back and sides

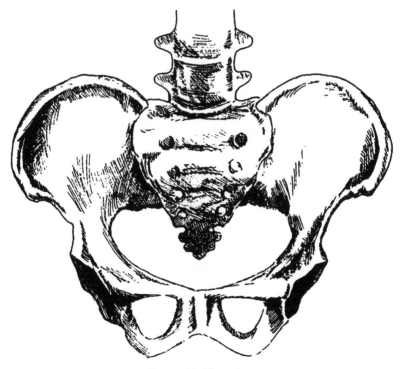

Figure 23. The pelvis

and lower in front. The wedge-shaped sacrum at the base of the spine forms the back of the bowl, and from each side of it a hipbone curves around to form the sides and the front. This structure supports the spine and absorbs the shock of movement from above and below. The pelvis plays a pivotal role in every movement of the trunk or the legs and is central to a dancer's posture and placement.

The Structure of the Hips

Each hipbone consists of three bones fused together — the ilium, the ischium, and the pubis. The crest of the ilium is the bony ridge you feel in the "hands on hips" position. The ischia are our "sitting-bones"; they form the lower back part of the bowl, while the two halves of the pubis meet in front to form the "crotch." The hip bones connect with the sacrum on either side at the sacroiliac joint, so completing the bowl. The exceptionally strong ligaments binding these joints cause the structure to move as one entity: the pelvis.

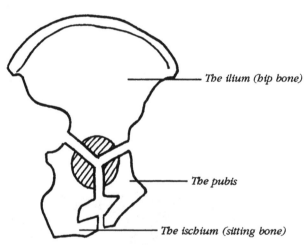

The ilium (hip bone)

The pubis

The ischium (sitting bone)

Figure 24. Each hipbone consists of three bones fused together

Just above the sitting-bones, on each side, is the round cavity of the hip socket, or acetabulum, which receives the head of the femur, or thigh bone. It is in this ball-and-socket joint that the all-important

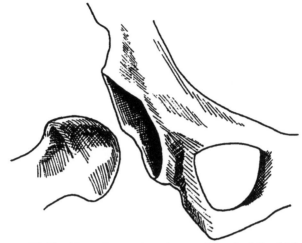

Figure 25. The hip socket receives the round head of the thigh bone

turnout is initiated, and it is here that the weight of the upper body is supported in the pelvis and transferred in a vertical line to the knees, ankles and feet. Surprisingly, dancers are often rather hazy about the exact location of their hip joints. If you draw a straight line up from your

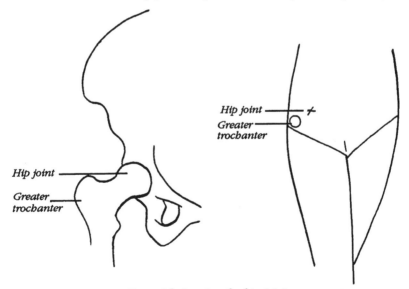

Figure 26. Locating the hip joint

knee to your groin, you will be pointing at your hip joint. The bones you can feel at the sides of the pelvis at a slightly lower level are the greater trochanters, which are protrusions on the upper part of the thigh bone. The greater trochanters are the site of many muscle attachments, causing us to feel movement initiating here, and so to mistake them for the hip joints. *But the two hip joints are no more than six or seven inches apart, on the front of the pelvis.*

Several ligaments bind the head of the femur into the hip socket, the most powerful being the *iliofemoral,* or *Y-shaped,* ligament. These ligaments limit an excessive range of motion at the hip joint, thus making a vital contribution to the stability of the upright posture. In

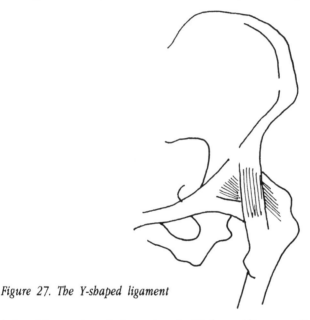

Figure 27. The Y-shaped ligament

doing this good work, however, the Y-shaped ligament limits the turnout and the backward extension of the leg, to the frustration of the dancer.

Flexibility in the hip joint is of great importance in all dance technique, influencing not only the turnout but also the ease of leg extensions. Properly performed, the traditional classical exercises slowly increase the suppleness of the hip, but not as much, alas, as some of us would wish. Success in this endeavor is directly related to age; the pre-teen body is highly amenable to change, though strength must be carefully cultivated along with flexibility. Once the dancer reaches the teenage years, the soft tissues around the hip joint are increasingly intractable. The dancer commencing instruction at a late age needs a naturally flexible hip joint if the training is to lead to a performing career.

A further discussion of the hip joint can be found in the chapter on turnout, begining on page 49.

Placement of the Pelvis

The placement of the pelvis directly affects the curve of the lumbar spine, which in turn affects the curves of the other spinal areas. It also affects the position of the femur in the hip socket, which, in a chain reaction, has a bearing upon the knees, ankles and feet. Thus the position of the pelvis —or of the hips, as dancers more commonly say — affects the functioning of the entire body.

Dancers are sometimes surprised at the way in which the movements of the pelvis are designated, as their kinesthetic sense leads them to feel the movements initiating in the crotch. Anatomists, however, describe the movements of the pelvis from the top of its front rim, so that when you drop your hip bones and stick out your tail, the pelvis is said to be tilting forward. Conversely, when you flatten your back and tuck your tail, the pelvis is said to be tilted back. Both of these aberrant positions are highly undesirable.

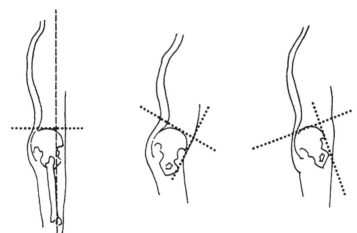

The centered pelvis   The forwardly tilted pelvis   The backwardly tilted pelvis

Figure 28. The placement of the pelvis affects the spinal curves

The forwardly tilted pelvis, usually accompanied by flaccid abdominal muscles, results in a hollow back (in anatomical terms, lordosis). It causes a compensatory increase in the thoracic curve, which results in a protruding rib cage and impaired breathing. The vertical line of gravity is disturbed so that the weight is no longer transferred through the center of the hip joint. The lower back is also under stress, and extensions of the leg in all directions are diminished. Even more destructive is the tucked, or backwardly tilted pelvis, which occurs almost invariably in response to the instruction "grip your buttocks." The lamentable effects are all-pervading. The reversal of the curve in the lumbar spine causes the other curves to flatten excessively, reducing the spine's flexibility and capacity for absorbing shock. Again, the vertical line of gravity is disturbed. The ligaments are strained, and the muscles of the thigh are overworked in their endeavor to prevent the knees from flexing. The results are often overall bodily tension, bulky thighs, and, owing to their relentless contraction, large buttock muscles.

The dancer must find a correct centered placement for the pelvis. The hip bones are lifted in front, while at the back the sacrum is directed strongly downward. (The sacrum, mind you, not the sitting-bones —this is no occasion for fuzzy thinking.) The buttocks are held high on the legs, while the lumbar spine remains elongated, as already described. The line of gravity, seen from the side, passes through the center of the hip joint and continues through the center of the thigh into the knee.

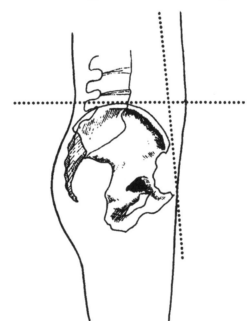

Figure 29. A dancer must find the correct centered placement of the pelvis

As the pelvis moves into its proper alignment, just the necessary amount of contraction occurs in the abdominal muscles and in the lower fibers of the buttocks. The upper fibers of the hamstrings, just under the buttocks, will also feel taut. This muscle action occurs naturally as a result of the proper placement of the pelvis; the right muscles *must* work if the bones are to be moved into the correct alignment, and they will continue to work properly to stabilize the structure in that position.

The image of the pelvis as a bowl is a very useful one for dancers, and it is unfortunate that most drawings do not capture its three-dimensional form. We are left with an impression of a flat bone with many complicated protuberances. Visualize your pelvis as a bowl that is being tilted from the rim; you will more easily feel the correct vertical placement.

Square Hips? In Battements Tendus and High Leg Extensions

When one leg is disengaged from a closed position, an important tenet of ballet training is that the hip crests should remain level and square to the front. This principle is open to misinterpretation and bears investigation.

Anatomists tell us that in the average person pure hip movement (movement of the femur in the hip socket), with no involvement of the pelvis and the spine, is limited to 60 degrees in the forward movement, 45 degrees to the side, and 15 degrees to the back.[9] But the finished dancer is not an average person; the ligaments would have been stretched over years of training, and in all likelihood were long to begin with. Even so, the dancer's advantage is not as great as one would expect. In an experiment carried out on professional dancers, kinesiologists Ryman and Ranney[10] have shown us that we cannot hope for even as much as 90 degrees of pure hip movement as the leg is raised to the front. The increase in range of motion to the side and back will be correspondingly modest.

That most basic of movements, the battement tendu, is a good point at which to begin an examination of the principle of square hips. In tendus to the front and to the side, the pelvis should remain uninvolved, with the hip crests absolutely level and facing square to the front. This rule also applies to a tendu to the back from first position, as in a rond de jambe. Its application is particularly important in this exercise, which has as its purpose the continuous rotation of the head of the femur in its socket, an action that gradually increases the flexibility of the hip joint.

In a tendu to the back from fifth position, however, unless the dancer is possessed of an unusual turnout, a slight horizontal rotation of the working hip occurs if the leg is to remain turned out and be directed to its proper position behind the center of the supporting foot (which, when the leg is raised, will be behind the spine). The hip crests must remain level, though the hip of the supporting leg will be slightly forward of that of the working leg The dancer minimizes the rotation as much as possible, for reasons we will examine shortly. This position of the pelvis is

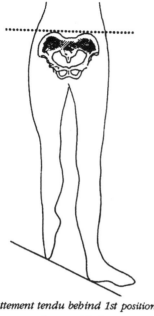 

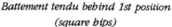

Battement tendu behind 1st position   *Battement tendu behind 5th position*
(square hips)   *(slight opening of the hip)*

Figure 30. The hips in battement tendu to the back

often referred to as "opening the hip" and is disallowed by some teachers, who place their priorities on the symmetry of the trunk and the ease of the spine in preference to the turnout or the exact direction of the working leg. In all positions, the shoulders should remain level and square to the front, and the rib cage should appear to be undisturbed.

As the working leg is raised past the point of pure hip movement, the pelvis, and with it the spine, enters into the action.

In an extension to the front, despite conventional teachings to the contrary, the pelvis begins to rotate upward in front and the lumbar spine flattens as the leg is raised.[11] This movement is disguised, however, by the fact that the upper body remains undisturbed and the lumbar spine elongated, thanks to continued stretching in the thoracic spine. There should be no hint of collapse between the ribs and the pelvis. At 90 degrees and above there will be a slight backward movement of the shoulders to offset the forward movement of the leg, an anatomical fact that is made into a stylistic feature in many methods of training. Visually, the movement of the pelvis is unnoticeable.

In the extension to the side, the pelvis tilts sideways in response to the raising of the leg. Even in a 90-degree extension of the leg, the lumbar spine has a considerable sideways curve. It remains elongated,

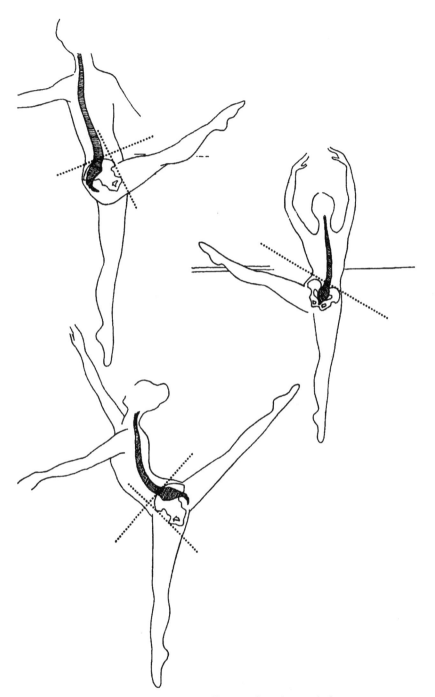

Figure 31. Leg extensions and their effect on the pelvis and the spine

however; there should be no shortening of the waist. The tilting of the pelvis is quite visible, but again our eye is led astray by the position of the upper body, which gives the illusion of more freedom in the working hip than actually exists. As far as possible, the head, shoulders and rib cage retain their vertical alignment over the supporting hip, knee, and foot, though inevitably there is an inappreciable sideways shift of the upper body to offset the working leg. Any noticeable shifting, however, is apt to give a visual impression of a lifted working hip. Again, it is the good work of the thoracic spine that makes this alignment possible.

As the leg is raised to the back in that all-important arabesque position, the pelvis begins to tilt forward and is almost horizontal when the leg reaches 90 degrees. It is prevented from any hint of collapsing onto the supporting leg by strong work in the abdominals. As the leg goes higher, the open-hip position is necessarily increased, though the hip crests must remain level. The lumbar spine is bent as it would be in a deep backbend.

The previous chapter on the functioning of the spine included a discussion of the importance of involving the lower thoracic spine in this backbend, so that there is no overly sharp angle in the lumbar area. Since the lumbar area has virtually no ability to rotate, the lower thoracic spine is also responsible for whatever rotation of the pelvis is necessary to keep the leg turned out and behind the spine.

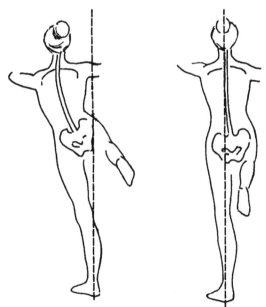

Figure 32. Alignment of an arabesque, viewed from the back

Then the thoracic spine has more work to do. Other vertebrae must spiral the opposite way to orient the shoulders and rib cage to the front and keep them level. There must be absolutely no sideways shift of the ribs or the shoulders in this position. *It is to minimize the load on the spine that we restrain the opening of the hip as much as possible.* Nevertheless, it is anatomically impossible to execute a high arabesque, and to get it turned out and directly behind the spinal column, without some opening of the hip.

It now becomes clear that the pelvis has a considerable role to play in all leg extensions, though it is *always in response* to the raised leg, *never in anticipation* of it. It is equally clear that the position of the upper body is of great importance in masking the movements of the pelvis. It would seem, at the very least, that "square shoulders" and "square ribs" should be included in our habitual vocabulary, and that "square hips," while useful as an image, should not be taken too literally once the early stages of training have been mastered.

Postural Muscles of the Hip

In cooperation with the abdominals, the muscles that form the buttocks establish the placement of the pelvis.They are the gluteus maximus, gluteus medius, and gluteus minimus, collectively known as the *gluteals.* The *deep outward rotators* also lie in the gluteal region. These muscles all arise at various points around the pelvis and are inserted into the region of the greater trochanter of the femur. The *tensor fasciae latae* acts in conjunction with the anterior fibers of the gluteus medius and so is included in this group.

The gluteus maximus is the most superficial muscle in the gluteal region; it is also the largest and most powerful. It originates from the top of the pelvis and from different points of the pelvic area, including the sacrum and the coccyx. It is inserted into the thigh bone just below the greater trochanter and into the fascia running down the outer side of the thigh. The many different points of origin enable different areas of the muscle to act independently of one another.

The gluteus maximus acts as an extensor of the hip joint, bringing the pelvis and thigh into line when the trunk has been bending forward or when the thigh has been flexed. This muscle plays a prominent role in jumps, as the dancer straightens the legs in the air, recovering hip alignment after the flexion of the plié. Together with the hamstrings (described on page 60), the gluteus maximus also initiates all battements to the back and, because of its different areas of insertion, can play a role in both abduction (away from the midline of the body) and adduction (toward the midline of the body) of the thigh. The gluteus

Figure 33. The gluteus maximus

maximus is a powerful outward rotator of the thigh, especially in its lower fibers—those in the vicinity of the sitting-bones. There is some controversy, however, about the deliberate contraction of this part of the muscle in achieving and maintaining turnout (see page 55).

Lying underneath the gluteus maximus and two-thirds covered by it, the *gluteus medius* covers the greater trochanter like a cap. This muscle also produces different actions in its different areas. The anterior, or front, fibers—those not covered by the gluteus maximus — are strong inward rotators as well as abductors of the thigh. The posterior, or back, fibers reinforce the gluteus maximus in outward rotation and in extending the hip joint. It is essential for the dancer to learn to isolate these areas from each other, as tension in the anterior fibers at the side of the hips will cause the thigh to turn in. Relaxing this part of the muscle is sometimes easier said than done;but remember, this is a two-way street: if the thigh bone is properly rotated in its socket, this forward part of the muscle cannot contract.

The gluteus medius is also a stabilizer of the pelvis; assisted by the tensor fasciae latae, it works strongly to support the body when the dancer is standing on one leg. It is the prime mover in abduction of the thigh.

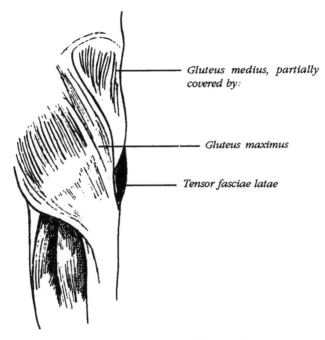

Gluteus medius, partially
covered by:

Gluteus maximus

Tensor fasciae latae

Figure 34. Diagram of hip muscles

Figure 35. The deep outward rotators

The *gluteus minimus* lies beneath the gluteus medius and reinforces its actions.

Almost completely covered by the gluteus maximus are six small muscles that are important stabilizers of the hip. They are the quadratus femoris, obdurator internus, obdurator externus, piriformis, gemelius superior and gemelius inferior. Together they are known as the *deep outward rotators*. They arise from different points around the sacrum and the lower part of the pelvis and are inserted into the greater trochanter of the thigh bone. These muscles also act as assistants in abduction and adduction of the thigh. Their action in outward rotation is very important to the dancer and is described in the following chapter on turnout.

The *tensor fasciae latae* is an egg-shaped muscle which is inserted into the band of fascia running down the outside of the thigh. When the muscle contracts, the fascia is tightened. Lying next to the gluteus medius, it cooperates with the latter in abduction and inward rotation of the thigh and helps to stabilize the pelvis. The tensor fasciae latae is also a flexor of the hip joint and an abductor of the thigh.

Questions For You To Answer:

Exactly where are your hip joints? Can you point to them?

How would you describe the shape of the pelvis?

How does the placement of the pelvis affect that of all other body parts?

What are the two principal muscle groups that hold the pelvis in its correct centered position?

In an arabesque, which part of the spine is working the hardest? Why?

5

Well Turned Out

The subject of turnout has long been a source of misunderstanding and contention, especially among those who do not fully understand the technical precepts involved. In sorting through the many misconceptions, we can be sure of one fact: though all dance techniques utilize a turned-out position of the legs to a greater or lesser degree, classical

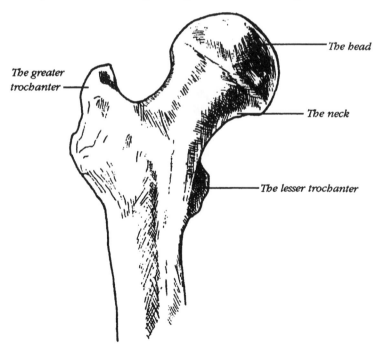

The head

The greater trochanter

The neck

The lesser trochanter

Figure 36. The thigh bone at hip level

ballet is *based* on the turnout; without it, the technique cannot exist. Far from being primarily an aesthetic concept, the turnout has a profoundly functional role. The well-turned-out leg makes a fundamental contribution to the stability, range of motion, mobility and strength of the dancer, as well as to the elongated shape of the muscles.

Our first task in examining this vital aspect of technique is to review the incontrovertible physical factors that *can* cause problems if they are not fully understood.

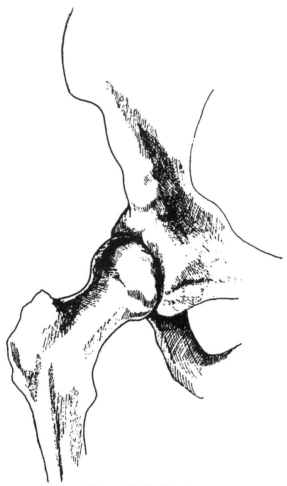

Figure 37. The hip joint

Factors Determining the Range of Turnout

At hip level, the femur, or thigh bone, is composed of a head, a neck and two bony protuberances, the greater and lesser trochanters. The round head fits snugly into its cavity on the front of the pelvis, forming a ball-and-socket joint that would have almost unlimited freedom of movement, and consequent lack of stability, if it were not braced by very strong ligaments holding the ball in the socket. The iliofemoral, or Y-shaped, ligament across the front of the joint is the strongest in the human body. Its relative tautness varies in each individual and is a factor in the amount of turnout that can be attained.

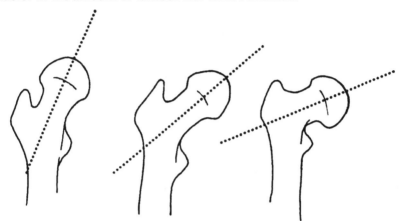

Figure 38. Individual variations in the angle of the femoral neck

Medical authorities tell us it is the bony structure of the hip that is the most important factor in determining the degree of possible turnout. First in importance is the shape of the femoral neck and the angle at which the head of the femur is inserted into its socket. Next is the orientation of the socket itself. Third on the list is the elasticity of the

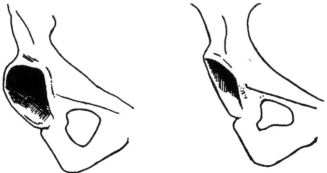

Figure 39. Orientations of the hip socket can vary considerably

hip ligaments, especially the Y-shaped ligament. Last comes the flexibility of the muscles around the hip and thigh, the only element over which we have any real control.

Dr. William Hamilton, writing in *Dance Magazine*,[12] adds that medical experts generally agree that changes in bony architecture can and do occur, the most rapid being from birth to the age of eight, with the process being mostly completed by the age of ten, though not totally finished until age sixteen. The prevailing opinion seems to be that ballet exercises may have an influence on the developing neck of the femur before the age of eleven, and that after this age no further change is possible. But we also know that bone growth can vary somewhat from child to child; sometimes a ten-year-old has the bone age of a teenager or, more often, an adolescent has an immature bone structure that may be amenable to some change.

Early training also brings about changes in the ligaments and soft tissues surrounding each joint. As the ligaments slowly begin to respond to the training, it is vital to remember that the bony structure must be protected by systematic strengthening of the reinforcing musculature. The potent ballet exercises will gradually and safely do their work of strengthening and stretching, provided they are induced to do so. The power of these seemingly gentle exercises makes it extremely unwise for a child to begin formal ballet training before the age of eight or nine.

On the whole, turnout is predetermined; the youngster with naturally turned-in hips will never attain the degree of rotation needed for safe execution of upper-level technique, and should not be forced. Fortunately, a process of self-selection seems to prevail at an elementary level. Children who find it difficult to progress to the intermediate level become frustrated or bored, and drop out. Teachers of the better-endowed children who continue their training must be assiduous in their efforts to coax young limbs into the fullest possible outward rotation while their bodies are still malleable. It is a slow process, but the goal must be clear and the aim constant if the full benefits of the training are to be reaped.

As the body matures, it is more difficult to increase turnout. The shape of the neck of the femur has been determined, and the ligaments are increasingly unyielding. The late starter who has professional aspirations in the field of classical ballet should already possess flexible hip joints and some degree of natural turnout. Without these, the student who reaches the upper levels of technical training must make constant compensations, with destructive effects on the body, especially on the knees.

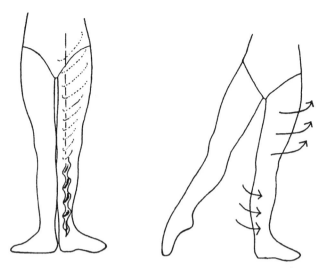

Figure 40. The turnout is a movement

The Turnout Is a Movement

The rotation of the thigh bone in the hip socket is a *movement*; it is an *action* the dancer takes, an action that must be learned and practiced. Visibly, the results take place in the thigh just below the pelvis, and continue into the knee, ankle and foot. The whole leg is rotated as one, and the relationship of each part to the other remains the same as when the leg is in a neutral position. A neutral position in standing does not necessarily imply parallel feet. There is a small natural turnout in the ankle that can be utilized and enhanced (see page 95).

The ability to maintain the turnout is as important as the amount of turnout attained and requires a good deal of strength in all the muscles concerned, strength that must be developed gradually, along with flexibility. In spite of the proliferation of warnings to the contrary, some teachers and many students persist in trying to force rotation from the feet, with little or no participation of the thigh and hip joint. As soon as movement commences, the turnout disappears. This practice also causes distortions throughout the whole body, affecting, among other things, the placement of weight, the tilt of the pelvis, and the curves of the spine. It is especially dangerous for the knees. Conscientious teachers need to keep a sharp eye out for students who determinedly adhere to this practice.

In their zeal to encourage maximum effort in the thighs, however, many teachers err in the opposite direction. They seem to have forgotten that, even in the tight-muscled bodies of some avocational students, although the turnout is *initiated* in the hip joint and thigh, the knee, calf, ankle and foot are dynamic partners in the action.

In a paper delivered with Martha Myers to the 1984 Olympic Scientific Congress in Eugene, Oregon, Dr. William Hardaker and Dr. Lars Erickson of Duke University Medical Center estimated that the 180-degree turnout is ideally achieved by 60 to 70 degrees of rotation in each thigh, with the remaining rotation taking place in the lower leg, principally at the ankle. They go on to point out that the full 70 degrees is rarely present even in the most distinguished professional dancers, yet trained dancers with a "natural" turnout usually have no difficulty in eventually achieving the overall 180-degree turnout without undue stress elsewhere in the body.[13]

The fully activated turnout is reflected throughout the entire body. In the same way that each leg rotates away from the other, the upper-level dancer will be familiar with the feeling of each side of the trunk widening from its central axis so that, from head to foot, one side of the body counteracts the other. The power thus generated is impossible to reproduce without a proficient turnout.

We hear a great deal about the potential dangers of the turnout, and there is no doubt that adult students in open classes and university courses should approach the matter with a clear head. Yet approach it they must, if they wish to benefit from their ballet classes. "Take care" must not be misconstrued as "do nothing." These dancers should learn to activate fully all the turnout they can command; in so doing, they will gain in strength and stability as they energize the entire body in the manner just described. They will also begin to see a change in the shape of their muscles, a welcome happening that is discussed in the following pages.

Up to a point, turnout can be improved by consistent steady work on the muscles of hip and thigh, though it is here that prudence must prevail. Too much enthusiasm in stretching the muscles around the hip can reach into the ligaments and the cartilage in the hip socket, risking damage to both. "Make haste slowly" is a good motto for all adult students.

The Turnout in Action

Since the turnout presents so many difficulties, why must we pay it so much attention? What are the benefits and advantages this troublesome action brings with it? First, observe the manner in which the range of motion for the legs is greatly enhanced by the simple device of moving the greater trochanter backward and getting it out of the way. The femur is thus given much more freedom in the hip socket, particularly in extensions to the side and to the back. The turnout allows the dancer to move with equal ease in any direction; in fact, most forms of dance employ a modified turnout for just this purpose. Stability is much increased because of the effect of the pull and counter-pull of the forces already discussed, and you will find more later in this chapter about the security as well as the mobility afforded by that greatest of all aids to the classical ballet dancer, fifth position.

Less frequently understood is the effect of turnout on the dancer's musculature. The radical change in a student's body over the course of a few years' training is often the subject of comment, yet gainsayers rarely give the credit where it is principally due: to the turnout. By altering the normal way the muscles function, the fully turned-out position of the legs plays a major role in developing the long, slender muscles of the ballet-trained dancer. Although it is true that a dancer's proportions are related to bone structure and cannot be altered, a beautiful musculature creates an illusion of harmony and compensates for many a flaw. On the other hand, when performed with perfunctory turnout, the powerful exercises of classical ballet can easily encourage overworked, chunky muscles, even in a beautifully proportioned body.

In advanced technique, with its constantly shifting equilibrium and lightning-swift changes of direction, ultimate demands are made on the turnout. Flexibility of the hips must match that of the spine in all twisting movements of the trunk, to relieve both the knees and spinal column of stress.

Muscles Activating the Turnout

There has been much disagreement among dance teachers about which muscles achieve and maintain the turnout. It now seems to be generally acknowledged that the powerful buttock muscle, gluteus maximus, should be used only very lightly for this purpose—only as much, in fact, as it is *automatically* activated by the action of turning out.

Although in its lowest fibers this muscle is a strong outward rotator of the thigh when the dancer is standing upright, and is almost always active to some degree whenever the leg is turned out, its principal mechanical function, in anatomical language, is to extend the hip, which means to align the pelvis and the thighs, and to realign them after they have been flexed. This muscle also contracts to produce any battement to the back; those lower fibers work strongly with the lateral hamstring to maintain the working leg in an arabesque. But in a situation where the hip is flexed, as in demi-plié, or at the height of a grand battement to the front or side, the muscle is forced to relinquish its hold. Dancers for whom gripping the buttocks is an article of faith can easily verify these statements: just stand in first position and place your hand on the lower part of the muscle. Tense with all your strength; then begin to bend your knees. Unless you are tucking your pelvis—an unpardonable sin—you will feel the muscle relaxing. Make the same test with a battement tendu to the back, and then swish through first position to the front. You can easily feel the release as the leg moves forward, and if you continue to raise the leg, increasing the flexion, the muscle will eventually be totally inactivated. If you are maintaining your turnout in the working leg, you are certainly not doing it with those lower fibers of the gluteus maximus.

It makes more sense to encourage the combined efforts of other muscles to establish and hold the turnout. The six small muscles collectively known as the deep outward rotators (see page 48), though normally not very powerful, are strengthened significantly by ballet training and play a major role in maintaining the turnout — provided the powerful gluteus maximus, which covers them, is not allowed to completely take over their job. Like many deep muscles in the body, you cannot ordinarily feel these small muscles, though it is possible to sense them. If you perform petit battement sur le cou de pied for a sufficient number of measures with a correctly placed pelvis and maximum turnout of the hips, you will feel a slight prickling sensation under your buttocks, a sensation caused by the outward rotators working hard to hold your turned-out thigh bone immobile, resisting the movement of your lower leg.

Ronds de jambe à terre is the exercise par excellence for increasing turnout. The circular movement of the leg rotates the head of the femur in its socket, which in turn goes to work on the ligaments and muscles around the hip, stretching them infinitesimally with the persistence of water dripping on a stone. Unfortunately, this exercise is rarely performed correctly from an anatomical viewpoint; too often it is used merely as an opportunity for pretty choreography at the barre. The action of rotating the thigh bone in its socket must be performed continuously, rhythmically, for many measures and, at an advanced level, at a brisk pace. Merrill Ashley, in *Dancing for Balanchine,* describes the master's requirements for the performance of a rond de jambe. The circle does not reach the tendu front or back positions, but makes an elliptical pattern which places the emphasis on the action taking place in the hip socket, rather than on the shape the foot is making on the floor. The hips must remain immobile, of course, and the toes of the working leg must be anchored firmly to the floor while they make the circle. We often performed the exercise this way in my student days. It may seem unusual to some of you, but it makes sound anatomical sense.

As you might expect, muscles of the thigh also act on the femur in either inward or outward rotation. These muscles are described at the end of this chapter. Remember the rule: stretch the inward rotators and strengthen the outward rotators.

Fifth Position

Fifth position is the ballet dancer's home base. By no means a position of the feet only, it is an attunement of the entire body. Fifth position is the smallest possible base for the weight of the body; freeing one leg requires no sideways adjustment and only a minuscule forward-backward adjustment is needed. It is the best possible position from which to propel the body in any new direction or into a combination of directions. The dancer standing in fifth position on straight legs is alerting the muscles of the thigh and calf that will be brought into action as soon as one leg is disengaged.

But perhaps the greatest value of fifth position is in plié, when the relaxed ligaments cause a slight additional turnout of the knee (see page 84), enabling the dancer to center the weight — or spine, or line of gravity — over this very small base. In this centering action the full effects of a good turnout are fully realized. An inadequate turnout will force the dancer to sit back in the plié (or, heaven forbid, allow the knees to fall forward) thus limiting, however slightly, full control and mobility. In motion the dancer continually returns to this centered position, if only for a split second, restoring balance momentarily before the quick transition into the next movement.

The small extra turning of the foot that is eventually required in order to take a secure fifth postion is described later, in the chapter on feet.

Claiming Our Heritage

The turnout is the foundation of ballet technique. Properly applied, it benefits the avocational dancer as much as the career dancer. By all means, let us handle it with care and banish any hint of related distortions in the feet, knees or spine. But then let us claim it as our legitimate heritage and use it up to the hilt — every degree we can mobilize.

The Muscles of the Thigh

Four groups of muscles control the actions of the thigh. For convenience they have been included in this chapter on turnout, though they function primarily in some other important capacities: they act on the pelvis to stabilize it, and they are responsible for flexion or extension of the leg at the hip joint. In each of the four groups there is at least one two-joint muscle acting on both hip and knee and, with the exception of the quadriceps, all make a contribution to either inward or outward rotation of the thigh.

The balance of each group with its opposite, or antagonist, group is a prime factor in controlling the stability of the pelvis when the dancer is standing on one leg. The adductors and the abductors, on opposite sides of the thigh, work against each other with balanced strength, while the hip flexors on the front of the thigh are only slightly stronger than the extensors on the back. (A ratio of 60:40 in the strength of quadriceps to hamstrings is considered normal.) The dancer who cannot "get up on his leg" probably has an improper balance in one of these muscle groups.

Weakness in any of these muscles not only limits the range of motion at the hip, but also places undue stress on the knee. Turnout will be diminished if the outward rotators are weak, though a much more likely problem is tightness in the inward rotators, the antagonists.

The *quadriceps femoris*, or *quadriceps extensor* as this muscle group is sometimes called, consists of four muscles (rectus femoris, vastus medialis, vastus intermedius and vastus lateralis) joining together to form a common tendon which is inserted into the patella, or kneecap. It is described in some texts as a muscle with four heads. The three vasti muscles arise from the femur in the vicinity of the greater trochanter but the principal muscle of the group, the rectus femoris, arises from the pelvis in the vicinity of the hip socket, making it a two-joint muscle, acting on both hip and knee.

Known familiarly in dance studios all over the world as "the quads," the main function of the quadriceps is to extend (stretch) the knee, and in this function it acts virtually alone, with some insignificant assistance from the tensor fasciae latae. The prime mover in this undertaking is the rectus femoris, but the vasti muscles take over in the final few degrees of stretch.

How happy we would be if we could confine the activities of the quads to this single function, as, of all the muscles in the dancing body, this one is the most susceptible to gaining unwanted bulk. But because of the origin of the rectus femoris, the quadriceps is also a powerful hip flexor, second in strength only to the iliopsoas. If there is any weakness in the action of the psoas or the other hip flexors, the rectus femoris takes over with alacrity. As well as increasing in bulk, an overactive quadriceps will diminish activity in the hamstrings, resulting in a loss of strength and efficiency in those important muscles.

The dancer uses several strategies to prevent unwanted bulk in the quadriceps. The turnout of the thighs is an important line of defense; it

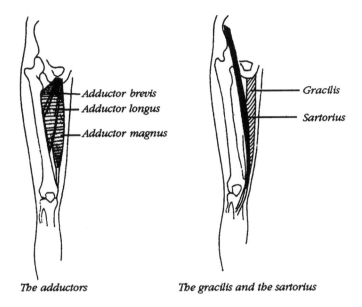

The adductors

The gracilis and the sartorius

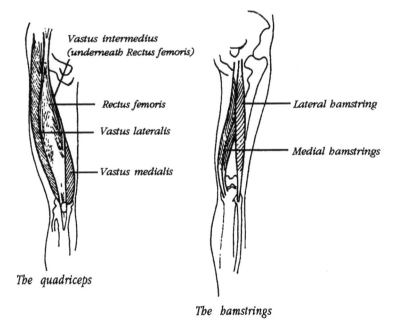

The quadriceps

The hamstrings

Figure 41. The muscles of the thigh

activates the other thigh flexors and places them in an optimal position to assist with flexion in battements to the front or the side. A correctly placed pelvis and habitual lengthening of the lumbar spine will facilitate proper usage of the iliopsoas which, as we have seen, is a principal flexor of the hip. As the leg rises, the rectus femoris, which has initiated the movement, gradually relinquishes its activity to the psoas.

Attention to the proper mechanics of the plié is important, too. On the downward movement, strong abdominals and a stable pelvis will absorb some of the pressure as the quadriceps contracts *eccentrically* to resist gravity. On the way up, a good push into the floor activates the calf muscles and the hamstrings and helps to minimize the "grabbing" of the rectus femoris as it contracts *concentrically* during the movement. Efficient use of the feet will relieve all these muscle groups of undue strain in landing from high jumps.

It is not just in pliés that the quadriceps acts in eccentric, or lengthening, contraction to resist gravity; the same contraction occurs as the leg is lowered from a raised position in front or to the side. The bunching of the thighs in such movements is a fairly familiar sight. It is usually caused by a foreshortening of the leg as it lowers, hiking up the hip and causing the muscle to clench as it contracts. This foreshortening can be prevented by a prompt recovery of the turnout, which has probably been partially lost at the height of the flexion, and by encouraging the hamstrings to participate in the movement. Imagery is a great reinforcement: "feel the inside muscles lengthening," and "draw a line with your toe, way out in space," are two favorites that work particularly well.

The quadriceps is the only major muscle group of the thigh that does not contribute to either inward or outward rotation.

The muscles at the back of the thigh are universally known as the *hamstrings.* In the turned-out position of the legs, these are the "inside muscles" to which teachers so often refer. They are long muscles, arising in the area of the sitting-bones, underneath the gluteus maximus, and running the entire length of the thigh. There are three of these muscles, but to all intents and purposes they act as two. The two muscles running down the inside of the thigh, with long tendons inserted below the knee into the tibia, are known as the *medial hamstrings.* The outside muscle is known as the *lateral hamstring;* its tendon is inserted into the fibula, just below the outside of the knee.

The two-joint hamstring muscles are the prime movers in flexion of the knee. They also act with the gluteus maximus and posterior fibers of the gluteus medius to extend the hip, bringing the pelvis and thighs into alignment. Their action in this respect comes into play in any movement where there has been flexion at the hip — in returning the leg from a battement, for example, or most notably in jumps after the flexion of the plié. The hamstrings also act with the gluteals in backward extension of the leg. Every battement to the back, every arabesque, is initiated by the hamstrings and the gluteals.

The lateral hamstring has an important role to play in accomplishing and maintaining turnout. By helping to turn the outside of the thigh backward, it works with the adductors as they bring the inside of the thigh forward. The controlling action of the lateral hamstring is especially strong at the point of its insertion into the fibula. In arabesque or any battement to the back, it becomes the principal muscle of the thigh to hold the turnout of the working leg, assisting the gluteals and the deep outward rotators. The medial hamstrings are inward rotators; turnout is restricted if they are tight.

Weak and malfunctioning hamstrings encourage inappropriate work in the quadriceps; by the same token, improper usage of the quadriceps results in weakness in the hamstrings. A good balance between these two muscle groups is of prime importance. Incorrect positioning of the pelvis, lordosis (hollow back) and faulty placement of weight are all conditions which, separately or together, will contribute to weakness in the hamstrings, as the traditional exercises will be performed without engaging these muscles sufficiently.

Figure 42. Initial position for stretching the hamstrings

Tightness in the lower fibers of the hamstrings, which pass behind the knee, will prevent the quadriceps from fully stretching the knee in a développé, and will limit flexion at the hips in a cambré forward, making it impossible to complete the movement. The hamstrings are not easy muscles to stretch, but the traditional exercises designed for the purpose will eventually reward a persistent dancer. Keep in mind the lesson of the stretch reflex, and remember, too, that a relaxed muscle stretches more readily than a tightly contracted one; ambition, therefore, must be tempered with reason.

The anatomical names of the hamstring muscles are the *biceps femoris* (lateral), and the *semimembranosus* and *semitendinosus* (medial).

The flat, ribbon-like *sartorius* muscle is also a two-joint muscle, arising at the top of the pelvis and running diagonally across the thigh and around the inside of the knee, culminating in a tendon which is inserted into the tibia, or shin bone, of the lower leg. The longest muscle in the body, the sartorius participates in flexion of the hip joint and outward rotation of the thigh, making it active in all battements to the front or to the side. It is a strong stabilizer of the knee in plié.

The muscles running down the inside of the thigh (when you are standing with parallel feet) are known collectively as the *adductors*. They arise in the vicinity of the pubis and, with the exception of the gracilis, are all inserted into the thigh bone. The *gracilis,* the only two-joint muscle in the group, is also the only inward rotator. It is inserted into the tibia, adjacent to the sartorius.

The principal function of the adductors is to draw the legs toward each other, an action that takes place continually when the dancer is in motion. These muscles are also outward rotators and flexors of the hip joint. Some authorities give the adductors the primary role in producing and holding turnout, but this is a minority opinion. The work of these muscles in presenting the inside of the thighs forward, though, is constant and important. The role of the adductors as flexors is enhanced in the turned out position of the legs, particularly as the leg is raised to fourth position front. The anatomical names of these muscles are *adductor brevis, adductor longus, adductor magnus, pectinius* and *gracilis.*

The *iliotibial tract* is a band of deep connective tissue, part of the *fascia lata* that runs down the outside of the thigh from pelvis to knee. It is controlled by the egg-shaped muscle, the *tensor fasciae latae,* which is inserted into this band and tenses it. The tensor fasciae latae works cooperatively with the anterior fibers of the gluteus medius. These muscles abduct the thigh and are also powerful inward rotators; if tight, they will effectively prevent turnout. An over-developed, rigid tensor is a very difficult muscle to stretch, and many dancers have found it necessary to enlist the aid of a masseur in this undertaking.

Although "sitting" in the hip can be produced by imbalance in any of the opposing muscle groups (or even improper work in the ankles), weak abductors, especially the tensor fasciae latae, is the most frequent cause. This muscle group is one of the very few that is not well served by

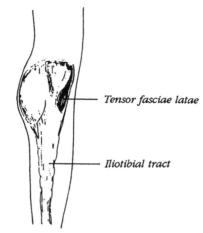

Figure 43. Diagram of iliotibial tract

traditional ballet exercises; the almost constant outward rotation of the thigh is apt to impede the development of strength in the inward rotators. Parallel grands battements to the side, preferably performed lying on the floor, is an effective strengthener of these muscles. Some innovative ballet teachers have added exercises performed in parallel positions to their warm-up at the barre, but probably the most useful strategy is for the dancer to leave the turnout behind when the studio door closes.

Figure 44. Strengthening the abductors

Questions For You To Answer:

What are the four factors that determine our ability to turn out in the hips?

Why is the turnout so important? What are the benefits it affords?

Is turnout confined solely to the hips?

What is the value of fifth position?

Name (in ordinary English), or point to, some of the muscles that accomplish the turnout.

Point to some muscle groups that, if tight, will prevent turnout.

6

Above the Waist

A sensitive and expressive use of the arms, exquisite hands, a mobile upper back, an open, unstrained chest, the tilt of the head, the glance of the eyes —these are qualities that mark the seasoned professional. They are the characteristics immediately noticed by onlookers, neophytes and experts alike. The emerging dancer with an eloquent port de bras, especially the young woman, immediately attracts favorable attention. She is perceived as talented, and until she should prove otherwise her development will be undertaken with special care.

It is sad, then, that so much attention is given these days to training below the waist, and so little to the most naturally expressive part of the body.

This neglect is especially regrettable when we consider that in order to develop a responsive, well-functioning upper body, it is not necessary for students to spend hours of extra time practicing special skills. Once the arm positions have been established, correct alignment of the ribs and shoulder girdle, together with attention to the free use of the arm in its socket, will achieve the intended objective as we go about the ordinary business of the ballet class. The earlier such correct usage is established the better, as nothing is more difficult to alter than a long-standing pattern of tension and rigidity in the upper body, arms and hands.

The Rib Cage

The anatomical name for the rib cage is the thorax, yet it is seldom used, so apt is the familiar "rib cage." Looking like a cage hanging on the spine, this elastic structure is made up of arches of bone, twelve on either side, connected at the spine to the thoracic vertebrae. In front,

65

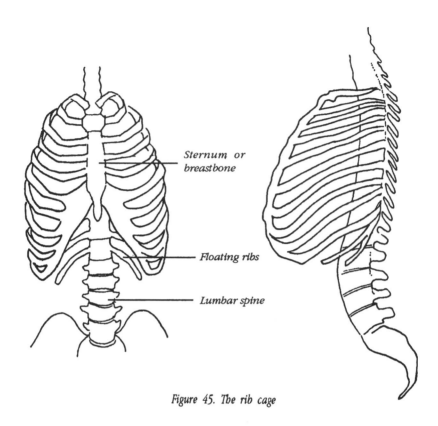

Sternum or
breastbone

Floating ribs

Lumbar spine

Figure 45. The rib cage

seven of these pairs are joined by their cartilage to the flat narrow bone
called the sternum, or breastbone. Three other pairs merge into each other
and then up into the sternum; the two lower pairs are free, or "floating."

The rib cage is a pliable structure capable of withstanding great stress,
and it contains our breathing apparatus. The elasticity of the cartilage
joining the ribs to the breastbone enables each rib to move somewhat
independently —an important factor, as a flexible thorax is a basic
necessity for efficient breathing. Rigid or constricted chest muscles
restrict this flexibility, causing shallow breathing, which, in a chain
reaction, adversely affects the movements of the entire spinal column.

If I had to pinpoint a single prevalent fault in otherwise well-trained
dancers today, it would probably be the alignment of the rib cage. The
protruding rib cage seen in so many ballet students, and even in some
professional dancers, makes some degree of rigidity a foregone conclu-
sion. This false position also distorts the spine, shortens the muscles in
the back, and disturbs the important relationship of the ribs to the pelvis.
It is frequently accompanied by a strained high chest: thrust-back shoulders,

stiffened neck and tense, contracted muscles. Sometimes this distorted position is deliberately adopted by inexperienced students in an effort to simulate the open shoulders and elongated neck of the classical dancer. Or, more often, it is a response to the exhortation to pull up.

In the proper position of the chest, the tips of the shoulders remain undisturbed while the top bone of the sternum is gently raised and directed forward, without strain, thus raising the top three or four ribs. The lower, more sloping, ribs should be left in place so that they are free to function fully and naturally in breathing. They should not be used as a scaffold, propping up a rigid chest. The shoulder girdle sits easily atop this structure.

"Open your chest" is a directive that is easily misinterpreted. It is the rib cage that you should feel to be opened—widened, equally back and front, away from the central line of gravity running through the trunk.

"Lift up your ribs," and "stretch your ribs," are commands that should be banished from every ballet class. Most dancers are frontally oriented and can be relied upon to lift up the *front* of the rib cage, tensing the chest and shortening the back. No matter how slight this action is, its results are counterproductive. Neither is it profitable for the teacher to poke and prod at the rib cage in correcting the dancer's placement. The resulting improvement, though immediate, is apt to be temporary. For lasting results the correction should be made in the spine itself.

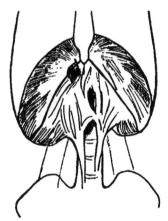

Figure 46. The diaphragm, the principal muscle used in breathing

A Muscle of Respiration

A large muscle shaped somewhat like a mushroom cap, the *diaphragm* separates the abdominal and thoracic cavities. (The thoracic cavity is the space enclosed by the rib cage.) The dome of the diaphragm forms the floor of the thoracic cavity; its underneath side provides a ceiling for the abdominal cavity. Parts of the diaphragm are attached to the lower ribs and to the lumbar vertebrae.

The diaphragm is the principal muscle used in breathing. It is in constant motion, lowering when we breathe in and moving upward again when we breathe out. As it lowers, the lungs expand to fill up the thoracic cavity, making the action of the diaphragm something like that of a pump. It is assisted by muscles called the intercostals, which occupy the space between the ribs and which cause the rib cage to inflate and deflate with each breath. The abdominal muscles also take part in the process; if you place one hand on the abdomen and the other on the ribs and breathe steadily, you can feel all this action taking place.

Faulty breathing can have a marked effect on a dancer's technique. It manifests itself in strains and tensions throughout the trunk, most noticeably in the muscles of the shoulder girdle, neck and jaw. We must provide the diaphragm with the environment it needs in order to function with optimal efficiency. Good muscle tone in the abdominals is one important requirement for good breathing, but probably the most essential ingredient is correct alignment of the trunk, especially between the ribs and the pelvis.

The Free and Easy Shoulder Girdle

The shoulder girdle consists of two pairs of bone, the shoulder blades and the collarbones, joined at the outer edge and hanging over the rib cage like a wide protective collar. Underneath each outer edge lies the shoulder joint, from which hangs the upper bone of the arm.

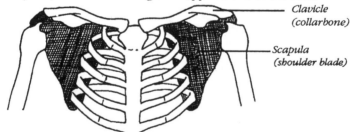

Figure 47. The shoulder girdle hangs over the rib cage

Considering the extreme mobility of the shoulder girdle, it ought not to come as a surprise to learn that this structure is almost completely free and independent of the rest of the trunk. Its only bony connection with the trunk is in front, where it is joined to the top of the breastbone For the rest of its support, the shoulder girdle depends on ligaments and on muscles suspending it from the head and neck from above, and other muscles attaching it to the spine and the rib cage.

The collarbones, or *clavicles*, are long bones that lie horizontally across the upper trunk. The shoulder blades, or *scapulae*, are flat bones, wide at the top but narrowing as they descend in a triangular shape as far as the seventh or eighth rib. Along the upper border of each scapula is a ridge, called the spine of the scapula, which serves as an attachment

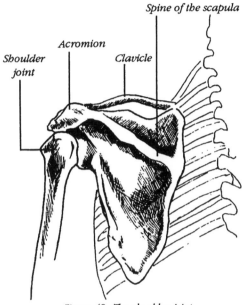

Figure 48. The shoulder joint

point for some important muscles of the back. Correctly aligned, the shoulder girdle hangs easily atop the rib cage, touching it only at a single point, the top of the breastbone. The tips of the shoulders point sideways and, when viewed from that angle, are congruous with the line of gravity.

The Shoulder Joint

The shoulder joint is formed by the long bone of the upper arm, the *humerus*, which is inserted into the *glenoid cavity*, a shallow socket on the shoulder blade. The joint lies directly beneath the prominent bone at the outer edge of the shoulder girdle, where each collarbone meets its corresponding shoulder blade. This bone, called the *acromion*, is sometimes mistaken for the shoulder joint, though it is actually quite separate. The humerus has a rounded head like that of the femur; the ball-and-socket joint thus formed is similar in structure to the hip joint, except that the socket is markedly shallower and consequently allows much more mobility. In fact, the shoulder joint is the most mobile joint in the body.

The arms have a considerable range of independent motion. They can be raised almost to shoulder height with no visible involvement of the shoulder girdle. The novice dancer can feel this isolation by placing a hand on the acromion and moving the arm backward and forward. The independent action of the arm in its socket below can be clearly felt.

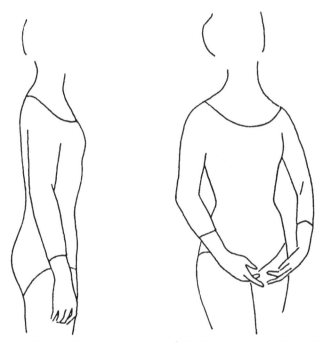

Figure 49. Once the correct alignment of the rib cage and shoulder girdle has been established, the classicial arm positions are easily assumed

When the shoulder girdle is correctly aligned and the lower tips of the shoulder blades are as widely spaced as possible, the arms hang easily in their respective shoulder joints. From this base it is an easy matter for the dancer to assume the classical arm positions.

The curved positions of the arms that form the foundation of the classical port de bras are often the subject of dispute. Some current schools of thought favor wider, higher, more open shapes than the traditional ones. Anatomically speaking, the arm socket faces outward and diagonally forward, favoring the more forward positions. Provided, though, that the upper arm is not held behind the shoulder joint, this matter can be considered a question of style.

The Mechanics of the Ports de Bras

The classical arm positions, through which all arm movements, in traditional technique, must flow, require an *inward rotation of the upper arm* whenever the arm is at or below shoulder level. As well as to preparatory, first and second positions, this rule applies to the lowered positions of demi-bras and demi-seconde, and to all the arabesques. The beginning dancer must learn to rotate the arms inward and outward without disturbing the shoulder girdle. When this action can be performed without involving the acromion, the student is ready to proceed.

It is in the second position of the arms that the mechanics of the curved position can most easily be understood, and it is this position that should be studied first. It is not an easy lesson to learn and requires much patience on the part of both teacher and student. The upper arm is rotated *inward* so that the elbow is softly lifted. The lower arm is then brought into alignment by *outward rotation*, with the wrist and hand completing a downward curve.

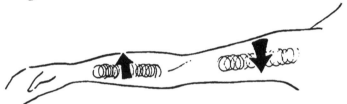

Figure 50. Opposing rotations of the arm in classical ports de bras

These opposing rotations are small, subtle movements and must be performed without any sign of strain. The rotation in the upper arm occurs in the socket and must not disturb the shoulder girdle. The outward rotation of the lower arm, which takes place at the elbow, is visually so slight as to be almost imperceptible.

The action of the upper arm, however, while not visibly affecting the shoulder tips or the clavicle, does engage muscles in the back that move the shoulder blades. As the rotated arms are raised toward the horizontal, there is a slight shift of position in the shoulder blades that is critical to a dancer's good carriage: the narrowed or pointed *lower* end of the blades begins to swing upward, outward, and forward along the rib cage, gently pulling the *upper* medial edge—the edge nearest the spine—down. Observe: with the lengthened spine and well-placed pelvis serving as a foundation, we can now see the rudiments of the open chest, lowered shoulders and apparently long neck so characteristic of the ballet dancer's stance. This has been achieved without strain or tension. The correct placement of the rib cage, shoulder girdle and arms has done its work; we are halfway home.

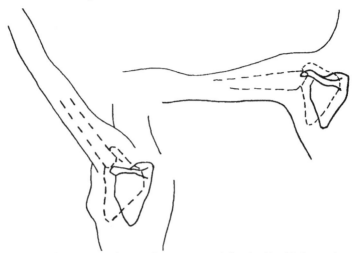

Figure 51. Diagram showing the movement of the shoulder blades as the arm is raised from preparatory position

As the arms continue to rise to fifth position, the movement of the shoulder blades increases until the sockets are facing diagonally upward, allowing the arms to rise freely while the inner edge of the shoulder blades is further depressed. At the same time there is a gradual change in the upper arm to an outwardly rotated position. This movement can be tricky for the student who has not mastered the lower positions. There must be no lifting of the shoulder girdle and no displacement of the rib cage, two conditions that require the necessary activity of the shoulder blades to be given a free rein. The muscles that cooperate to produce this action are described in the section at the end of this chapter.

As the arms are opened from fifth to second position, the change back again to inward rotation is a difficult one for the neophyte dancer, one that requires a good deal of attention from the teacher.

The erroneous but prevalent notion that there is no movement in the shoulders during ports de bras makes for poor imagery on the part of the dancer and can have an inhibiting effect on the freedom with which the arms are used. It is the *clavicle* that remains calm, giving the impression of immobility along the top of the shoulders. There is plenty of activity in the shoulder blades themselves every time an arm movement is made.

The dancer needs strength and flexibility in the muscles of the upper torso. These will gradually be acquired as training progresses, providing correct placement of the bony structure and proper usage of the arms have been established.

Muscles of the Upper Torso

Nowhere in the body is the interrelationship of muscles more marked than among those of the shoulders, back and arms. They lie in several layers, and some are divided into three or four parts, allowing one muscle to participate in a number of different, sometimes opposing, functions. No single muscle group acts without the participation of several others, the whole resulting in a complex symphony of coordination.

In the following pages I discuss only those muscles that most plainly affect the classical port de bras in its everyday performance in the ballet class. By limiting the scope of this study to the prime movers and to the basic port de bras, I hope to have made the material as digestible as it is useful. Needless to say, with this aim in mind, I have purposely omitted many muscles.

It may help to make the reading easy if you remember two anatomical terms that are certain to crop up: *adduction* (toward the midline of the body) and *abduction* (away from the midline of the body). It is also important to distinguish between movements of the arms (in the

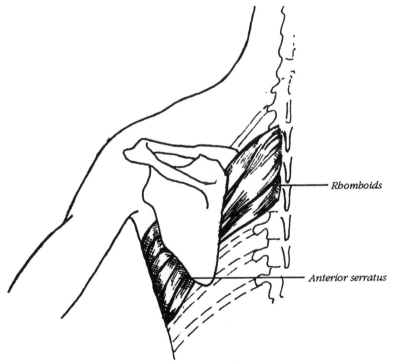

Figure 52. The rhomboids and the anterior serratus are antagonistic in their action

shoulder joint) and movements of the shoulder blades (part of the shoulder girdle), and to bear in mind that although the discussion refers to muscles on one side of the body, there is always a duplicate set on the other side. The spine is the dividing line.

The *anterior serratus* and the *rhomboids* are considered first because their antagonistic action is fundamental to the efficient functioning of the arms, though in fact their activity is confined to the shoulder girdle. These two muscles, lying on opposite sides of the shoulder blades, hold the blades in place against the rib cage. In so doing, the two muscles are assisted by muscles that cover them, the *trapezius* and the *latissimus dorsi*. The rhomboids (major and minor, treated in this book as a single entity) pull the shoulder blades in toward the spine; the anterior serratus pulls them outward, at the same time rotating them, positioning the socket for free use of the arms. This action is described and illustrated on page 72.

The fan-shaped *anterior serratus* arises in the ribs at the side of the body and is inserted along the entire inner border of the shoulder blade, sandwiched between shoulder blade and ribs. All muscles involved in forward, sideways, or upward movements of the arms

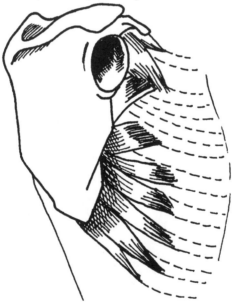

Figure 53. The anterior serratus viewed from the side

depend on the efficient functioning of the anterior serratus. The muscle acts on the lower point of the shoulder blade, moving it upward, outward or forward along the rib cage, changing the position of the socket so as to set the stage for the muscles responsible for moving the joint. From preparatory to first position, for instance, there is already a decided movement of the shoulder blades. As the arm rises above the horizontal, the anterior serratus becomes the star performer instead of the stage manager; the tilting of the socket is now the principal cause of movement. Dr. Werner Platzer, in *Color Atlas of Human Anatomy*, tells us that "Elevation, which may be a continuation of abduction, is due not to movement within the shoulder joint, but is produced by a rotation of the scapula."[14] The movement we can feel within the joint, apart from abduction, is the change from inward to outward rotation. In the early stages of the movement, the upper fibers of the trapezius offer some assistance in the undertaking by slightly pulling up the outer tip of the shoulder blade (in the vicinity of the acromion). As the arm completes its change to outward rotation (fifth position), the middle fibers of the trapezius are strongly activated to stabilize the shoulder girdle provided the anterior serratus is performing its task competently.

The action of raising the arms often raises the outer tips of the shoulders somewhat, depending on the degree of efficiency in the whole set-up. This circumstance is bothersome to some students whose muscles have not yet developed the fine coordination of the professional dancer, and who are determinedly trying to obey the instruction to "pull down your shoulders." However, the directive does not refer to the outer tips but to that part of the shoulder girdle in the vicinity of the spine. If this area is kept lowered, by pulling the muscles down all the way into the lower back, the aesthetics of the ports de bras will be satisfied in harmony with the natural mechanics of both bony structure and musculature in the area. If the shoulders are continually hiking up to the ears, however, something is not working properly, and ten to one it is the balance between the anterior serratus and its antagonist, the rhomboids.

The *rhomboids* arise in the thoracic vertebrae of the spine and they, too, are inserted on the inside of the shoulder blades, between blade and ribs. Their action is exactly the reverse of the anterior serratus. As well as pulling the shoulder blades toward each other, they work cooperatively with the latissimus dorsi to rotate the shoulder blades so that the socket is facing downward, making it possible for the arms to be moved backward.

Habitually contracted rhomboids interfere with the functioning of the anterior serratus; they also result in tight, rigid, elevated shoulders—the inward movement of the lower end of the blades raises the upper edge nearest the spine, thus elevating precisely the area of the shoulders that we wish at all costs to keep lowered.

Weakness in either of these muscles, but particularly in the anterior serratus, is one of the principal causes of "winged" shoulders—the shoulder blades have detached themselves from the ribs. Often these two conditions are combined, the shoulders being both tight and winged, a circumstance that is exacerbated, and indeed possibly caused, by that most harmful instruction, "pull your shoulders back," or even worse, "pinch a nut between your shoulders," an old-fashioned directive that can still be heard from time to time in ballet studios across the country.

In a well-functioning upper back the rhomboids are widely spaced, giving the anterior serratus the opportunity to slide freely along the rib cage and perform its task with maximum efficiency.

The *trapezius* is another muscle that acts on the shoulder girdle and only indirectly on the arms. It arises at the top of the spine and hangs like a cloak from the back and sides of the neck, draping the shoulders and continuing down to a triangular point at the twelfth thoracic vertebra.

The primary function of the trapezius is a static one: it is the most important muscle engaged in stabilizing the shoulder girdle. If you remember that the shoulder girdle has only one bony connection to the rest of the trunk, you can appreciate the importance of this function. Its importance is greatly increased in ballet technique as, with some assistance from the latissimus dorsi and the pectoralis major, this muscle is chiefly responsible for holding the shoulders down. In its active mode the trapezius is the prime mover in the arching of the head and upper back, and assists in turning and inclining the head. The upper fibers of the muscle raise the outer points of the shoulders; the lower fibers pull them down again after they have been raised. The middle fibers assist the rhomboids in pulling the shoulder blades backward and toward the spine. The independence of its upper, middle and lower fibers enables it to function in these diverse actions. The upper trapezius is a "tension muscle" without parallel. Bodily stresses owing to bad placement often manifest themselves first in the contraction of this part of the muscle; fear and anxiety are almost sure to be reflected here.

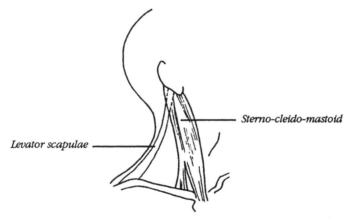

Figure 54. The sterno-cleido-mastoid and the levator scapulae

The *levator scapulae,* lying in the neck beneath the upper trapezius, is attached to the top of the shoulder blades and to the first four cervical vertebrae. As its name implies, it raises the shoulders, but its postural role is more important to the dancer—it stretches the neck if the shoulder girdle is stabilized. The levator scapulae also acts quite vigorously with the trapezius when bearing weight, as when the male dancer carries his partner on his shoulder.

The *latissimus dorsi,* the great muscle of the back, is the largest muscle in the body. It is able to act directly on both the shoulder girdle and the arms. It ascends from the crest of the pelvis, branching gradually outward, embracing the lower back and the ribs and clinging to the shoulder blades, before continuing its outward course to be inserted into each humerus. In this manner it connects the arms directly with the lower back; hence the ballet dancer's habitual carriage, with the lower back muscles strongly activated, has a direct bearing on the functioning of the shoulders and the arms. In its upper fibers, below the shoulder blades and branching toward the armpits, the muscle works to assist the trapezius in anchoring the shoulder girdle, relieving the trapezius of unnecessary tension. It assists in inward rotation of the arms and provides yet further stabilization of the shoulder blades against the ribs. The latissimus takes part in the stretching and backward bending of the spine, and it also pulls the arms backward so that the hands can clasp behind the back. It is especially active in arabesque, acting on both the arms and the arch of the back.

The *deltoid* acts directly on the arms. It covers the outer tips of the shoulders like a small cap, arising from the outer third of the clavicle, the spine of the scapula and the acromion, and is inserted in the upper part of the humerus. Its anterior, middle and posterior fibers all function independently, making it capable of many different and opposing actions—in fact, there is no movement of the arms in which the deltoid does not participate to some degree. The most important action of the deltoid is to abduct the arm: move it away from the midline of the body. All the curved arm positions in classical ballet involve abduction—the upper arm is abducted and rotated. Since in traditional ballet technique the dancer is constantly moving through these positions, the deltoid is continuously engaged. It is most active in raising the arm sideways, as from preparatory to second position, assisted by the biceps brachii, the big muscle of the upper arm. Together with the *pectoralis major* its anterior fibers draw the arm forward; its posterior fibers work with the latissimus dorsi in drawing the arm backward. The deltoid can also take part in both inward and outward rotation of the arms, and in adduction. Correct functioning of the shoulder girdle minimizes the work of the deltoid, an important consideration since, if overworked, the muscle

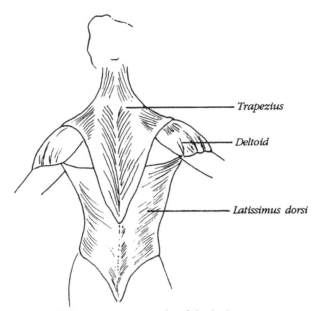

Figure 55. Some important muscles of the back

easily gains unwanted bulk. Except in the action of abduction, in which it is the prime mover, the deltoid should perform as an accessory muscle, and lightly at that. One of my colleagues describes it as the "quadriceps of the arms."[15]

The *pectoralis major,* the large muscle of the chest, arises from along the breastbone and the clavicle and the upper sheath of the rectus abdominis. It is inserted into the upper part of the humerus and is therefore able to act on both the shoulder girdle and the arms. This muscle is the prime mover in adduction of the arms. For example, the front arm in an arabesque is adducted. It assists in raising the arms forward and inwardly rotating them (first position). As the arms rise above horizontal, the pectoralis major works on the clavicle to keep the shoulder girdle lowered. The muscle participates in lowering the arms from fifth to second position, and works especially strongly against resistance. The male dancer lowering his partner from a lift calls upon all the strength the pectorals can muster.

A thin muscle situated beneath the pectoralis major, the *pectoralis minor* arises in the mid-area of the front of the rib cage and passes upward and outward, to be inserted, unlike the major muscle, on the inside of the shoulder blade, adjacent to the acromion. The pectoralis minor pulls the shoulder blades forward, acting as a counter to the trapezius, which pulls them back. A balance between these two muscles is an important factor in good placement of the shoulder girdle.

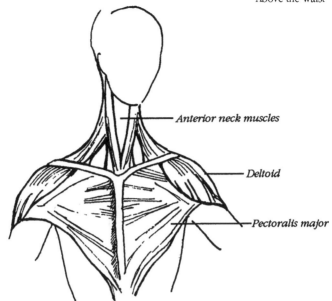

Figure 56. Frontal view of muscles acting on the shoulder and arm

Tightness in either of the pectoral muscles inhibits the arching of the back and contributes substantially to round shoulders.

The big muscle on the upper arm, the *biceps brachii*, is a two-joint muscle that acts on both the shoulder joint and the elbow. It arises in the shoulder blade in the vicinity of the arm socket and is inserted into the lower arm, below the elbow. It is an inward rotator of the upper arm, and because of its rotary action at the elbow, an outward rotator of the lower arm—exactly the way the arms are held and moved in all the below-shoulder ballet postions. This muscle participates in abduction of the arm and in moving it forward, as from preparatory to first posi- tion. With the assistance of a deep underlying muscle, it flexes the elbow. For the male dancer it is the prime mover in raising his partner overhead in a full arm lift; the pectoralis major assists in this action and then assumes the stronger role as the arms are lowered. The muscle is opposd by its antagonist, the *triceps brachii*, on the inside of the arm. The triceps adducts the arm and extends the elbow, as in an arabesque. It assists the pectoralis major in lowering the arms from fifth to second postion.

The *sterno-cleido-mastoid* arises from the sternum and the clavicle and is inserted into the mastoid process. This thick muscle passes obliquely across the front of the neck. The habitual stance of the ballet dancer, with elevated head and lowered shoulders, causes it to be more visible than it might ordinarily be, especially when the head is turned.

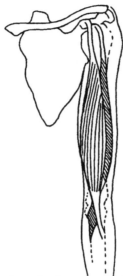

Figure 57. The biceps brachii acts on both shoulder joint and elbow

The sterno-cleido-mastoid acts with the trapezius to turn the head and bend it to the side, and its eccentric contraction helps to support the weight of the head in a backbend.

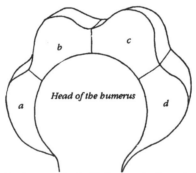

Four reinforcing muscles hold the arm in its socket and participate in either inward or outward rotation of the arm

Figure 58. The rotator cuff muscles

Four muscles collectively known as the *rotator cuff* muscles arise from the scapula and form a protective cuff around the shoulder joint. They stabilize the head of the humerus in its shallow socket. It is the strength of this stabilization that enables the arms to move safely with such freedom. Each of the rotator cuff muscles participates in either inward or outward rotation of the upper arm. One in particular, the *subscapularis*, is an especially strong inward rotator.

To sum up: of the muscles we have been discussing, the ones responsible for good placement of the shoulder girdle are the rhomboids, anterior serratus, trapezius, pectoralis minor, levator scapulae, and the latissimus dorsi.

The muscles that move the arms are the biceps brachii, pectoralis major, deltoid, triceps brachii, latissimus dorsi, rotator cuff muscles.

In preparatory position, the upper arm is inwardly rotated and slightly abducted. In first position, it is inwardly rotated, forwardly flexed and slightly abducted. In second position, the upper arm is abducted and inwardly rotated. In fifth position, it is outwardly rotated, slightly abducted and flexed. In all these positions, the forearm is outwardly rotated.

If the arms are held and moved in proper accordance with the precepts of classical ballet technique, they will be in harmony with the natural way the body is meant to function.

Questions For You To Answer:

What is the principal muscle used in breathing?

Why is the alignment of the rib cage with the pelvis so important?

Exactly where is your shoulder joint?

Why is the shoulder girdle so extremely mobile?

What part of your body will betray your fear and anxiety?

7

A Modified Hinge

The knee is the dancer's nemesis. To the unwary, it is an accident waiting to happen. The largest and most complicated joint in the body, it is designed to provide both stability and mobility, but hardly to withstand the punishing treatment it often receives in the dance studio. The demands we make on this joint have no parallel. We jump, turn, twist and balance in positions of ever-increasing precariousness, all of which require utmost strength and mobility from the knee joint.

Imprisoned as it is between the pelvis and the foot, the knee relies on correct placement of both for its stability. Maximum use of turnout in the hip socket is a necessity; a turned-out foot and turned-in thigh is a combination that is certainly going to cause trouble. In plié, the alignment of the knee directly over the center of the foot is mandatory at all times. Correct placement of weight through the ankle and into the foot is also essential. A rolled foot, for example, gives a nasty little twist to the knee that will eventually take its toll. Flexibility of both spine and hip joint is needed to relieve stress in the supporting knee in movements involving twisting of the trunk.

It takes a great deal of patience to learn something of the workings of this complex joint, yet even a rudimentary knowledge is of immense value, especially for the teacher. For once, the proverbial "good eye" is no substitute. The knee is an unforgiving joint; once injured it will continue to give trouble throughout a dancer's career.

The Structure of the Knee

The bony structure of the knee joint comprises the lower end of the femur, the upper end of the tibia and the patella. In layman's terms, these are the thigh bone, the shin bone and the knee cap.

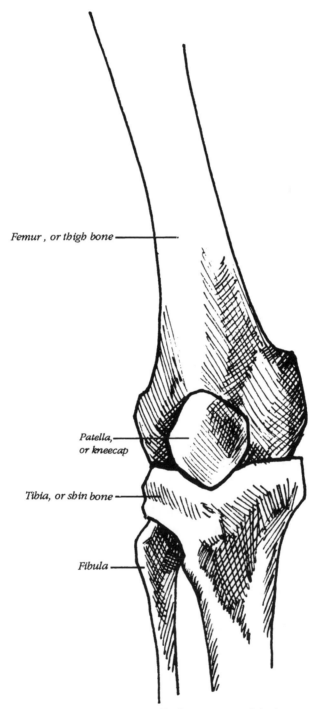

Femur , or thigh bone

Patella,
or kneecap

Tibia, or shin bone

Fibula

Figure 59. The bony structure of the knee

You have already been briefly introduced to the *femur* in our discussion of the hip joint. The longest bone in the body, it descends diagonally inward from its greater trochanter to form the upper part of the knee joint.

The *tibia* is the principal bone of the lower leg. It is somewhat smaller than the femur, yet it has more weight to support, so it is reinforced by the long slim fibula which is attached to its lateral, or outside, condyle. (A condyle is a projection at the end of a bone.) The fibula is not actually a part of the knee joint, but serves as a point of attachment for the lateral hamstring and some important muscles of the lower leg that act on the foot. One of the ligaments reinforcing the knee is also attached to the fibula.

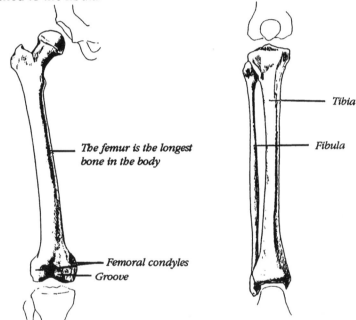

The femur is the longest bone in the body

Femoral condyles

Groove

Tibia

Fibula

Figure 60. The femur, or thigh bone

Figure 61. The tibia and fibula, bones of the lower leg

The condyles of the femur and the tibia are separated by two crescent-shaped discs of cartilage, the menisci, a familiar source of trouble to the dancer. "Torn cartilage" in the knee invariably means a damaged meniscus. The condyles of the femur are separated by a deep groove, which allows important ligaments to pass through the joint.

The *patella,* or knee cap, is a small triangular bone lying in front of this groove, protecting the femoral condyles. It is not attached to the

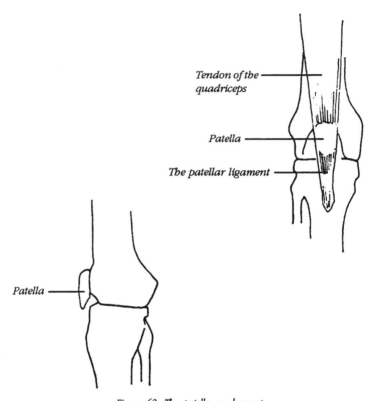

Tendon of the quadriceps

Patella

The patellar ligament

Patella

Figure 62. The patella, or kneecap

other bones, but arises in the tendon of the quadriceps muscle, which attaches to its sides and continues to its lower tip to become the patellar ligament, inserted into the tibia. Between the patella and the femur, a large sac of fluid, known as a bursa, prevents friction; a smaller bursa protects the front of the knee cap. "Jumper's," or "housemaid's," knee is caused by inflammation of the small bursa.

Unlike the hip joint, which derives its strength from its structure, the knee joint has to rely on the many strong ligaments and muscles that brace the joint and work collaboratively during movement. The ligaments that are of most interest to the dancer are the *medial* and *lateral collateral ligaments* and the *anterior* and *posterior cruciate ligaments*.

The medial (toward the middle) and the lateral (away from the middle) collateral ligaments run down the inner and outer side of the knee, respectively. The medial ligament extends from the inside

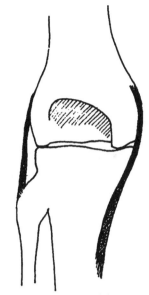

Figure 63. The collateral ligaments

femoral condyle to the inside of the tibia; the lateral ligament extends from the outside femoral condyle to the head of the fibula. These ligaments prevent any sideways movement of the joint when the leg is stretched.

You can best understand the location of the cruciate, or "crossed," ligaments by examining the sketch. The anterior (toward the front) ligament is attached at the front of the tibial condyle and passes

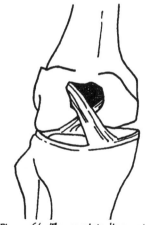

Figure 64. The cruciate ligaments

obliquely upward through the groove in the condyles of the femur, to be inserted in the back of the lateral femoral condyle. The posterior ligament travels the opposite path, from the back of the tibia to the front of the medial femoral condyle. Thus a cross within the joint is formed. The cruciate ligaments maintain the connection between the tibia and the femur, providing forward-backward stabilization. Muscles from the thigh and calf overlap at the knee, providing powerful reinforcement to the strength and stability of the joint.

Alignment of the Knee

The conformation of the knee becomes increasingly critical as the dancer progresses to the upper level of training. If you view the body from the front, you should be able to draw an imaginary line through the centers of the hip, knee and ankle joints. Viewed from the side, the line would pass through the center of the hip socket and continue down slightly forward of the center of the knee joint (because of the dancer's slightly forward stance) and on into the foot, just in front of the ankle.

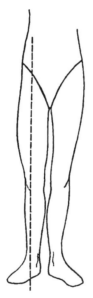 

Viewed from the front, a plumb line would fall through the center of the hip, knee and ankle joints

Viewed from the side, the plumb line would fall slightly forward of the center of the knee joint and just in front of the ankle

Figure 65. The alignment of the knee

There are four types of knee that fail to fall along such a line: knock knees, bow legs, tibial torsion and hyperextended, or "swayback," knees. If any of these conditions exist to a marked degree, they will affect the ability of the lower limbs to carry weight efficiently. In the case of the first three conditions, the alignment of foot to knee is incorrect, and the angle at which the thrust from the floor is taken is disturbed. Speed, elevation, balance and pointe work will all be impaired.

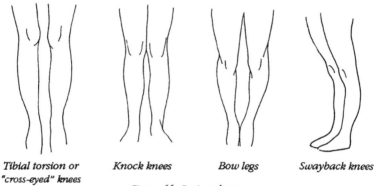

Tibial torsion or   Knock knees   Bow legs   Swayback knees
"cross-eyed" knees

Figure 66. Deviant knees

In the loose-limbed student likely to progress to professional training, though, a certain amount of swayback in the knees is almost inevitable. Dr. Werner Platzer, in *Color Atlas and Textbook of Human Anatomy,* tells us that in children and adolescents, "the leg may be overextended by about five degrees." A similar overextension certainly can be observed in most professional dancers. A small amount of swayback is not considered to be true hyperextension (genu recurvatum, in medical terms). The mechanism of the joint will not be affected, and the dancer needs to employ no special strategy to maintain control. The traditional rules of classical technique suffice, *provided they are understood and adhered to.* The dancer must stand on straight legs with well-braced thigh muscles and kneecaps that are lifted by the quadriceps, making a conscious effort to maintain the turnout and resisting any tendency to push back farther in the knees. The weight of the body must not be allowed to fall back into the heels. The alignment of the pelvis is crucial: "Groin over toes" is a useful correction. Any limbering exercise that further increases the stretch behind the knees should be avoided.

The successful management of a greater-than-normal degree of hyperextension depends largely on the strength of the supporting musculature and the intelligence of the dancer. The care and management of deviations is a subject beyond the parameters of this book and has been well documented in many writings.[16]

The Knee in Action

The movements of the knee are flexion and extension, supplemented by a small degree of rotation when the knee is bent. There is also an involuntary rotary movement that occurs at the final moment of straightening. The rotation is reversed when the knee begins to bend. This combination of movements makes the traditional comparison of the knee to a hinge something of an oversimplification.

In ballet, as in all forms of dance, motion is fueled by plié. It is essential for the safety of the knee joint that this pivotal movement should be performed *at all times* with correct alignment of knee to foot. We are all familiar with the wrenching accidents that can occur if the knee falls forward and inward when a dancer is landing from a jump. "Knees over toes" must be drilled into students from the first lesson, until it becomes an automatic action on the part of every dancer. Even then, fatigue and momentary carelessness can trap the unwary, as many of us know to our regret.

When the knee is bent the collateral ligaments are relaxed, so that side-to-side stability of the knee is entirely dependent on the bracing action of the muscles. The cruciate ligaments also relax somewhat as the knee is flexed, thus lessening the restraints and allowing some rotation to take place. On outward rotation these ligaments become unwound, allowing a little more movement than is possible on inward rotation, when they are twisted around each other. In plié the turnout of the entire leg is increased slightly by this ability of the knee to rotate somewhat when flexed, a circumstance that aids the moving dancer to pass through closed fifth positions with a well-centered spine.

The straightening of the knee follows a complicated pattern that we would do well to understand. Dr. Lulu Sweigard gives a clear description of this complex rotational movement:

> As the knee nears extension, the anterior cruciate ligament stops the movement of the outer femoral condyle, holding it steady while continued muscle action (of the quadriceps) for full extension results in inward rotation of the femoral condyles and menisci — as a unit—on the tibia (tantamount to outward rotation of the tibia)....*It is a locking of the knee without hyperextension.* [17]

To the dancer, the only visible evidence of all this action taking place is the pull of the quadriceps on the kneecap, but the occurrence, known to anatomists as *closure rotation,* is essential to the security of the ballet dancer, especially to the female on pointe.

The injunction "don't lock your knees" is puzzling to those of us who belong to a generation of dancers who were raised in the firm belief that a locked knee is of paramount importance to the dancer's stability. This contradiction seems to be a matter of semantics. In the present-day use of the word "lock", the directive is issued to prevent the dancer from pushing the knees back into a full extension with no concomitant bracing of the thigh muscles—a feat only too easy for most ballet dancers. Given without explanation, however, and as a general principle rather than as a correction, its consequences are apt to be slack knees and an insecure supporting leg, the quickest route to serious accidents. Make no mistake: in a normal knee, if the leg is properly straightened and the patella is pulled up by the quadriceps, as it should be, the collateral and cruciate ligaments will be taut, and the joint will be, anatomically speaking, locked.

But there is a big difference between a lock and a deadbolt. Excessive and unrelenting clenching of the quadriceps muscle in order to brace the joint and raise the kneecap is counterproductive. Correct though it is in its basic assumptions, the pulling up of the front of the thighs, like so many other good things, can be overdone by students who have reached an advanced level of training and have gained considerable strength in these muscles. Once the closure rotation has taken place, there can be no further movement in the joint. As we have already observed, any muscle contracted more than is needed to perform the task at hand will increase in bulk. And any joint that is locked to the point of rigidity by muscular contraction blocks the flow of movement.

The great ballet masters have always warned us about excessive tension of the knees, for a variety of reasons. In the 1950s, Tamara Karsavina insisted on the need for relaxation of the muscles when closing into the fifth position; in her book *Classical Ballet: The Flow of Movement* she emphasized the importance of this precept. A generation later Karel Shook, in his wise little book on elementary training, *Elements of Classical Ballet Technique,* wrote of the anatomical impossibility for most students of standing in a correct fifth position with pulled-up thighs. He advised us to "relax (the quadriceps) until the action of the temps is begun."

Be that as it may (and most teachers will have their own ideas on this point), the well-being of the knees will always be a preoccupation of any knowledgeable dancer. It is in helping you to assess just the right amount of muscle action needed to maintain stability of the knee that the good eye of the teacher comes into its own.

The Knee in Disorder

There is no doubt that dancers have more ways than one of punishing the knee joint. "Sitting" at the bottom of a grand plié or allowing the knees to fall inward when rising from one will put unwarranted strain on the ligaments. The traditional practice of commencing the barre with grand plié has been called into question by movement educators, who believe the exercise is too demanding to be performed at the outset of class, and who advocate a change in the order of the barre. For teachers in commercial studios with open classes and large numbers of students, this may be a wise precaution. But it negates much of the exercise's value, which is to bring the legs into a state of elasticity by galvanizing all the muscles, and to check into the feeling of placement and turnout in relation to each other at the beginning of the class. The simplistic notion that the main purpose of the exercise is to strengthen the quadriceps is partially responsible for the controversy. Performed correctly and in moderation, the grand plié is not stressful to the knees, though it certainly offers plenty of opportunity for faulty execution and must be regarded as an upper-level exercise. If dancers cannot be relied upon to warm up before class, a set warm-up routine is always good practice.

Other sources of potential trouble are not too difficult to pinpoint. Ronds de jambe a terre performed with a relaxed knee will do some damage fairly quickly, as the rotational stress will occur in the knee instead of in the hip joint. The damage caused by sickling in or out when on pointe is not confined to the ankle; the knee takes its share of the stress. It is fair to say, though, that the indiscriminate forcing of the turnout is responsible for more serious knee problems than any other factor. A particularly brutal practice is that of planting the feet in 180-degree turnout in plié and then slowly stretching the knees. The outward

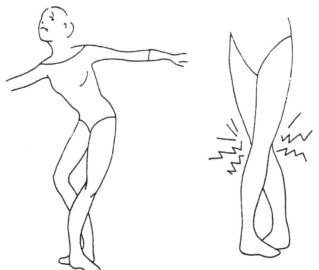

Figure 67. Forcing the turnout

rotation decreases progressively during the stretch, and this painful practice places unwarranted stress on the ligaments responsible for the safety of the joint. It also achieves nothing of value, as the hip joint remains unaffected.

This principle being understood, there is an exercise frequently given at the barre in elementary classes which needs some rethinking. It is: battement tendu, close in fifth position plié, slowly stretch. Obviously intended as a precursor to the indispensable "tendu demi-plié" (which in turn sets us up to land and take off again with correct placement of weight), this exercise is not as innocuous as it may seem. If the closing is into a loose fifth, the exercise has little value; if a proper fifth is taken, the knees can be stressed as described above. A better solution is: battement tendu, close plié, repeat the tendu, close on straight legs. This strategy minimizes wear and tear on the knees while still giving both teacher and student plenty of opportunity to concentrate on centering.

The knee is a complicated piece of bodily machinery; one that, not without cause, induces a pervasive sense of apprehension in the minds of all dancers. A little real knowledge can provide a large amount of protection and, of equal importance, peace of mind.

Muscles Acting on the Knee

The task of strengthening and stabilizing, ordinarily a secondary function of muscles, assumes primary importance in the case of the knee joint, particularly in plié, when the ligaments are mostly relaxed. The overlapping muscles of the thigh and calf are then mainly responsible for the safety of the joint, as well as for producing movement. Most of these muscles are two-joint muscles, acting also on either the hip or the ankle joint.

Extension (stretching) of the knee is produced almost exclusively by the large *quadriceps* muscle which covers the front of the thigh, its tendon attached to the patella. The main function of this muscle is to extend the knee, but one part of the muscle (the rectus femoris) also acts as a flexor of the hip. The thigh muscles were described in Chapter 5; a discussion of the quadriceps can be found beginning on page 58. The quadriceps also acts in eccentric contraction to resist gravity in every plié, making it of prime importance in the safe use of the knee, especially in landing from jumps. A weak or malfunctioning quadriceps is almost guaranteed to lead to knee injury.

Flexion (bending) of the knee is produced by the *hamstrings*, with assistance from the *gracilis* and the *sartorius*. These two-joint muscles have also already been described (see pages 60-62).

The *gastrocnemius*, the large calf muscle in the lower leg, participates

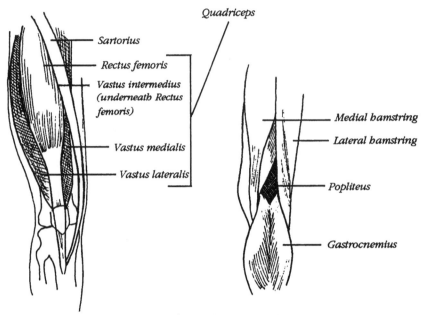

Figure 68. Muscles acting on the knee

in knee flexion, but as its action on the ankle is of more interest to the dancer, it is described in the following chapter on feet.

The *popliteus* is a small muscle at the back of the knee, the action of which is confined solely to the knee joint. This muscle is important in the beginning stages of flexion. The instruction "begin the plié from the back of the knees," which is not heard as frequently today as it once was, makes good sense.

Questions For You To Answer:

Which muscle is mainly responsible for the safe usage of the knee? What are the two principal ways in which it acts on the knee?

The turnout in the knee increases slightly when we are in plié. Why?

How can this extra turnout be abused?

What are some other common faults that can lead to knee problems?

8

The Bottom of It All

To most balletgoers, the aristocratic foot of the dancer is the distinguishing feature of classical ballet. Strong and supple, and as sensitive as a hand, the foot is used by the dancer in a manner that, to the eye of the observer, departs distinctly from the ordinary mechanics of movement.

To a dancer the feet are servants of the first rank. Like the tiny feeder roots of a tall strong tree, on which the health and well-being of every leaf and branch depend, the feet are a source not only of strength and support, but also of propulsion and shock absorption and, most importantly, of perception. Sensations relayed from the foot inform the rest of the body of the level of its support, its trajectory, its orientation to space, and countless subtleties that are reflected instantly in every movement. It is no exaggeration to say that the quality of a dancer's movement is directly related to the level of sensitivity in the use of the feet.

Good training slowly strengthens the feet and makes them supple; indifferent training can quickly weaken their structure. In *Anatomy and Ballet,* Celia Sparger has pointed out that "the foot which functions correctly when it is weight-bearing will function correctly in movement." This piece of wisdom, to which every experienced teacher will reply, "Of course," is too often neglected, especially in the early stages of training. Constant vigilance and persistence on the part of both teachers and students are needed for good working habits to be established.

The Structure of the Foot

The Ankle

The malleoli are two bones commonly called the ankle bones. The inner malleolus is a projection of bone on the inside lower end of the tibia; the

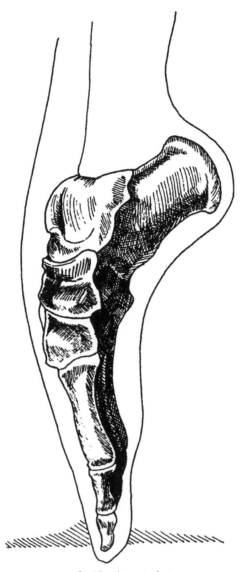

Figure 69. The dancer's foot

outer malleolus is at the lower end of the fibula. The talus, an important bone that transmits the weight of the body to the foot, fits into the cavity formed by the malleoli. The ankle is a hinge joint, capable of flexion and extension only. Sideways or rotational movements you may think are in the ankle actually take place in the joints of the foot. The talus, also known as the astragalus, is tightly embraced by the two malleoli, preventing sideways movement in a normal foot. In a position of extreme extension, as on pointe, there is a minuscule amount of sideways movement owing to the shape of the talus; the ballerina sometimes utilizes this imperceptible movement to maintain stability in prolonged balances on pointe.

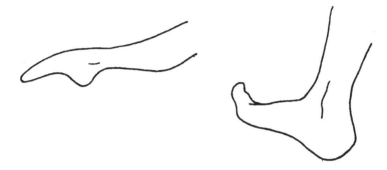

Figure 70. A dancer needs a flexible ankle

Many ligaments bind the lower end of the tibia and the fibula, contributing to the stability of the ankle joint. Two important ligaments bind the joint itself: the *internal lateral ligament*, or deltoid ligament, which is one of the strongest ligaments in the body and almost impossible to rupture, and the much weaker *external lateral ligament*. The latter is the "sprain ligament," the sprain occurring when the foot rolls over toward the outside and twists, rupturing the fibers of the ligament.

The serious student set on a professional career needs certain God-given gifts of physique, none of which is more important than flexibility in the ankle joint. The understandable emphasis given to the significance of a natural turnout is apt to overshadow that of a pliable ankle. A lack of mobility in this joint directly affects two elements central to dance technique: the plié and the "pointing" of the foot. A tight foot with limited flexion results in a shallow demi-plié, the enemy of all dancers. A foot lacking in extension at the ankle joint will probably have its ability to propel lessened, and it certainly will not support the female dancer's weight when she is on pointe. Neither, of course, will it develop the graceful curve so aesthetically desirable in the pointed foot.

Movement in the ankle joint can be limited by several factors. Tightness in the ligaments binding the joint or in the calf muscles inhibits mobility, but should gradually release as training progresses. However,

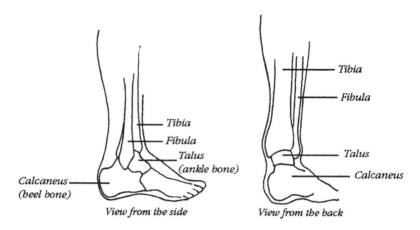

Figure 71. *The structure of the ankle joint*

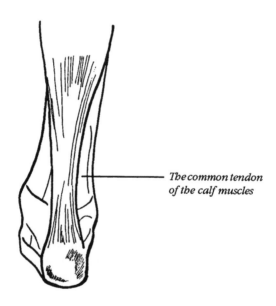

Figure 72. *The Achilles tendon*

if the problem is one of bone-on-bone in the interaction among the talus (ankle bone), the calcaneus (heel bone) and the tibia (shin bone), there is little to be done. We cannot alter bone structure and any forcing not only will be useless, but also possibly harmful. A short Achilles tendon is another almost insoluble problem. The Achilles tendon, the common tendon of the calf muscles, is inserted into the heel and is one of the toughest in the body. If it is tight, trying to stretch it can be an exercise in futility. This type of foot has limited flexion at the ankle, but its extension is unimpaired. Fortunately, a true shortening of the Achilles tendon is rather rare. The problem is more likely to be tightness in the calf muscles themselves. Exceptionally tight calf muscles may not respond to traditional exercises and may require special supplementary conditioning work, or even help from a physical therapist.

Up to a point, the female dancer with a shallow plié can be taught to utilize the amount she has, while the male with too little arch can learn to disguise his shortcomings provided his jump is not affected. Should the coin fall the opposite way, though, a professional performing career in any of the dance disciplines is an unlikely prospect. An experienced teacher or physical therapist, manually flexing and arching the student's foot, can usually tell whether there is sufficient resilience to respond to advanced training.

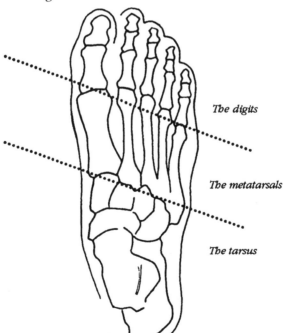

The digits

The metatarsals

The tarsus

Figure 73. The bony structure of the foot

The Foot Itself

The bony structure of the foot can be divided into three parts: the tarsus, the metatarsus, and the digits, or toes. A brief study of the sketches and comparison with your own foot will clarify the arrangement of the twenty-six bones that make up these areas.

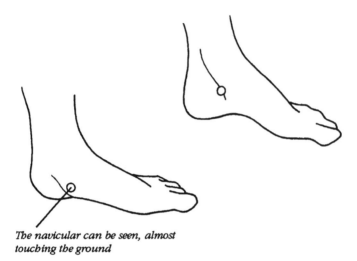

The navicular can be seen, almost touching the ground

Figure 74. The rolled foot

The tarsus forms approximately the back half of the foot and consists of the following seven bones:

The calcaneus is the heel bone, above which is the talus. The talus is described on page 96 as part of the ankle. The cuboid is in front of the calcaneus on the outer side of the foot; the navicular is placed on the inside, along with the three small cuneiforms. The navicular has a small knobby protrusion on the inner side which can be clearly seen, sometimes almost touching the floor, when the foot is rolled.

In the forefoot, the metatarsals are the five long bones leading to the toes, or digits. With the exception of the big toe, each digit comprises three small bones, or phalanges; the big toe comprises only two.

This structure forms a series of arches that give the foot its strength, flexibility, qualities of propulsion and ability to withstand the shock of weight transmission. For our purposes, it is useful to consider these arches as aspects of the two principal ones, the longitudinal and the transverse arches.

The Arches of the Foot

The longitudinal arch runs the length of the foot from heel to toes. It has a medial (inside) and a lateral (outside) aspect. The inside of the arch is higher than the outside. It is this area of the arch that can collapse in a pronated, or rolled, foot: the talus and the navicular can be pushed out of position, or the metatarsals can sink, seriously impairing the ability of the foot to act in propulsion and in shock absorption. In addition, the weight is no longer transmitted correctly through the ankle, and this has repercussions in the placement of the entire body.

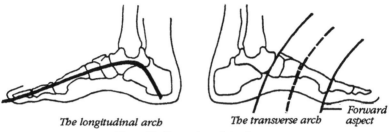

The longitudinal arch   *The transverse arch*   Forward aspect

Figure 75. The arches of the foot

The transverse arch runs across the foot. It has a forward aspect, where the metatarsals meet the toes, which is sometimes known as the metatarsal arch. It also can give way, usually in sympathy with some degree of collapse in the longitudinal arch. Then the heads of the metatarsals sink, pinching the nerves between the bones and causing much pain. In a healthy foot the metatarsal arch is flexible and resilient; when weight-bearing, it flattens and lengthens, but as soon as the weight is taken off the foot, the arch obligingly reappears. In the rear aspect of the arch, at the middle of the tarsus, the bones form only half a dome. When the feet are placed together in a parallel position, the domes form a complete arch.

This entire formation is bound together by many ligaments and by the tendons of the muscles of the lower leg, which pass through the ankle joint and are inserted into various parts of the foot.

The Foot in Action

The muscles that produce the movements of the foot all arise in the leg below the knee, with the exception of the big calf muscle, the gastrocnemius, which arises above the knee and acts on both the knee and the foot.

The muscles that flex the ankle and the toes are situated on the outer side of the front of the leg and pass around or in front of the ankle joint.

The calf muscles and their deep underlying assistants extend (stretch) the ankle joint and point the toes. In this task they are assisted by muscles on the sole of the foot that act on the toes to complete the curve and form the arched foot of the ballet dancer. These muscles, self-contained in the foot itself, are known as the intrinsic muscles of the foot. They play a vital role in every action the foot is called upon to perform.

Classical ballet training is uniquely endowed with movements and exercises to develop strength in the intrinsic muscles: the forceful brushing and striking of the floor in battements tendus, dégagés, frappés, and the like; the spreading and pressing action of the supporting toes working against the resistance of a correctly centered, or "pulled up," ankle; the instantaneous contraction of the sole every time the foot leaves the floor; the relevé in its several forms. All these movements do their strengthening work with utmost effectiveness, provided they are conscientiously performed.

The Weight-bearing Foot

In a well-functioning foot the weight is placed on three points: the heel, and the big and little toes. There is more weight on the forward part of the foot, especially in the early stages of training before the turnout is consolidated, but the heel must still take its fair share. A straight line can be drawn vertically through the center of the knee and the center of the ankle, and on into the second toe.

The toes are elongated and pressed firmly down along the floor, providing an anchor from which the ankle is actively pulled up. A lively ankle sends a message to the entire body, but until the spreading and

Figure 76. Energy in the toes

pressing actions of the toes are established, the ankle cannot be other than a passive partner in the process.

The spreading action of the toes is an accomplishment in itself for a student in a first pair of ballet shoes. It is vital that the joints between the phalanges (those little bones in the toes) remain extended; there must be no hint of "clawing" of the toes.

It is invariably the weight-bearing, or supporting, foot that suffers damage when the foot is wrongly used. Every teacher is familiar with the ubiquitous rolled foot which occurs when the weight is placed on the inner border of the foot. This problem is far more common than its opposite, inversion, or "sickling," when the weight is placed on the outside of the foot. The inverted foot is often very strong, and because a slight sickle is automatic in a powerful push-off, the jump is unimpaired. Apart from being aesthetically unacceptable, however, the sickled foot presents a danger in pointe work and in landing from jumps. Too much strain on the outside of the foot, the site of the vulnerable external lateral ligament, may eventually result in a sprained ankle. It is not for nothing that this ligament is known as the "sprain ligament."

The Foot and the Turnout

It cannot be repeated too often that turnout must be initiated in the hips, yet the foot and the ankle do have an active and gradually escalating role to play. In the early stages of training it is essential that first priority be given to spreading the toes and holding the ankles in the correct centered and pulled-up position. Until these conditions have been met, all turnout should be restricted, even in a student with naturally flexible hips.

As training progresses, the strengthening of muscles in the lower leg and foot must be intensified. The specific exercises acting on these muscles, especially the battements tendus, must gradually be increased in number and vigor of execution. The toes must be trained to be strong enough to adhere to the floor like magnets, with no buckling of the phalanges. Correct alignment through the center of the ankle to the second toe must be maintained at all times. The turnout, initiated in the hips and maintained by muscles in the lower back and thigh, now also makes demands on the muscles of the lower leg and ankle.

Then there comes a time when a slight extra turning of the foot is required in order to take a secure fifth position. By now the muscles in the lower leg and ankle have gained sufficient strength for the dancer to hold the foot in its proper alignment in the new position. As the body's weight is slightly rearranged around its center, imperceptible adjustments occur in the placement of the entire body: head, spine, pelvis and knees all respond to the new position. The foot itself has been well prepared for this extra work in non-weight-bearing positions, when the stretch along the inside of the foot into the big toe has been emphasized. Celia Sparger has observed that if this extra turning of the foot is insisted upon before the muscles have strengthened, or if it should prove to be physically too difficult for the individual student, the muscle balance of the foot will be disturbed, with most unhappy results. At the same time, we know that the younger the student is when this stage is reached, the more easily the ligaments adjust, one more reason to favor an early start.

Pointe Work

When a young dancer dons her first pair of pointe shoes, all the work of the last several years comes together—or falls apart. She has arrived at a stage where no more accommodations are possible. Placement should have been consolidated, turnout established, and the muscles of the feet strengthened. The arch will have been developed sufficiently for the student to take a good three-quarter pointe, with the ankle bone over the toes.

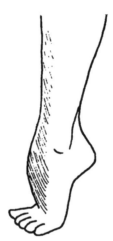

Figure 77. A three-quarter pointe with a well-developed arch

If the training up to now has been unsound, every deficiency is revealed and results in problems. The well-trained student, on the other hand, experiences little new challenge in the use of the feet. The stance on full pointe is similar to that on three-quarter pointe. There is a slight adjustment of balance and centering, more pronounced for the long-backed dancer with a naturally low center of gravity. It takes a modicum more strength to maintain stability on the smaller base, and the muscles in the soles of the feet have to work slightly harder to point the toes, but essentially pointe work is a logical extension of the lessons already learned. A possible exception is the student with a hyper-mobile ankle joint who may have managed to control it up to this point, but who now finds that she lacks the extra strength needed to prevent sickling in or out when on full pointe. Sad to say, if this type of foot has not already responded to the strengthening process, it is unlikely to improve.

There is no doubt that rather short toes of almost equal length are an advantage, and that a big toe that is either much longer or much shorter than the rest is a nuisance; but, providing the muscles have been strengthened, the student who can take a proper three-quarter pointe should not experience any major difficulties. There are as many different ways of coping with minor deviations as there are different pairs of feet: choosing the right shoes undoubtedly ranks first in importance. *The Pointe Book,* [18] by Janice Barringer and Sarah Schlesinger, gives invaluable advice about every aspect of these matters.

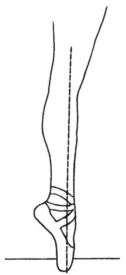

Figure 78. The alignment of the foot on pointe

The transition from three-quarter pointe to full pointe can be made in two ways, and a dancer must be able to use both. The smooth roll up involves a change in the vertical line of gravity; the springy "snatch" pulls the toes under the centered line. In either case, the movement goes through the demi-pointe both during the relevé and on the descent, and that imaginary line still falls through the centers of the knee and ankle, and on into the second toe. The toes, strengthened by three or four years of training, remain elongated.

The dangers of putting young children on pointe before the bones of their feet have begun to ossify have been so well documented that it hardly seems necessary to mention it here. Yet perhaps too much attention has been paid to the possible damage to the feet and not enough to the impairment of other parts of the body, especially the knees, which are likely to be placed under stress. It takes an expert eye on the part of the teacher to make a decision about readiness for pointe work. The musculature of the entire body should have been developed sufficiently to hold the correct alignment of the trunk, hip, knee and ankle. Dr. William Hamilton, writing in *Dance Magazine*,[19] relays to us the delightfully commonsense viewpoint of Balanchine, who remarked that children should not be put on pointe until they have the strength and training to do something when they get up there.

This would usually be after about three or four years of quite intensive work, so the dancer would necessarily be at least eleven or twelve years of age. A delay of several more years would do no harm, provided the training has not been interrupted during that time and the necessary strength has been developed. It must be emphasized, though, that the once-a-week ballet class is no preparation for this specialized work, and students who do not have professional aspirations would be well advised to get on with the dancing and forego the temporary thrill of pink satin pointe shoes.

Capezio/Ballet Makers, as one of this firm's many services to teachers and dancers, has printed a brochure entitled "Why Can't I Go On My Toes?", an excerpt from Celia Sparger's *Anatomy and Ballet*. Teachers with "problem parents" should avail themselves of a few of these excellent reinforcements.[20]

Muscles of the Lower Leg and Foot

In discussing the intricate action of these muscles, it has sometimes been necessary, for the sake of clarity, to use anatomical terms. Some of these terms have already been introduced, but they have a particular meaning when applied to the foot.

The following table can be used for reference:

PLANTAR FLEXION	Pointing the foot, extending the ankle
DORSIFLEXION	Flexing the foot, turning up at the ankle
INVERSION	Raising the inner border of the foot

EVERSION	Raising the outer border of the foot
ADDUCTION	Turning the forefoot inward
ABDUCTION	Turning the forefoot outward
SUPINATION	The combined action of adduction and inversion
PRONATION	Its opposite, abduction and eversion

We refer to a supinated foot as "sickled"; a pronated foot in a non-weight-bearing position is "winged." When a pronated foot is weight-bearing, we refer to it as "rolled."

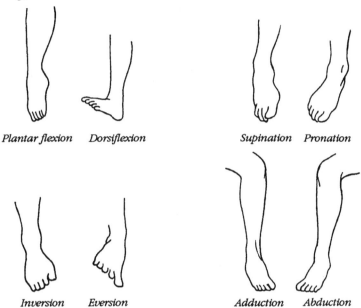

Plantar flexion   Dorsiflexion   Supination   Pronation

Inversion   Eversion   Adduction   Abduction

Figure 79. The movements of the foot

Movements of the ankle joint and the foot are performed by the four layers of short muscles on the sole of the foot, and by muscles which, with one important exception (the large muscle of the calf), arise in the lower leg, pass through the ankle joint and are attached to some part of the foot. The names of all these muscles are enough to give any dancer anatomical indigestion, and to complicate matters further, they nearly all have at least two actions on the foot. It is not necessary for you to be able to name them, but you will profit from a clear understanding of their actions.

The *gastrocnemius*, the big calf muscle, arises above the knee and ends in the Achilles tendon, which is inserted into the heel. Its underlying partner, the *soleus*, also ends in the Achilles tendon, but arises beneath the knee. Thus the gastrocnemius is a two-joint muscle, acting to bend the knee and to extend the ankle, while the soleus confines its action to the ankle. These muscles are the principal actors in plantar flexion (extension) of the ankle. They extend the ankle and raise the heel off the ground and are of critical importance in relevés and jumps.

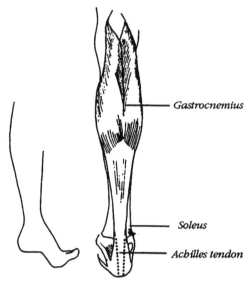

Figure 80. The gastrocnemius, the big calf muscle.
It covers its underlying partner, the soleus

The tendons of three deep-lying muscles under the calf wind around the inside of the ankle joint and attach themselves to various bones on the underside of the foot. They continue the action of plantar flexion into the foot itself. One of these is attached to the navicular and cuneiform bones; another acts on the four outer toes, assisting the short muscles of the sole; the remaining one works on the big toe. All these muscles act to supinate (sickle) the foot and are counteracted by strong work in another group, the peroneals. They also help to support the arch and to maintain the proper relationship between the front and back part of the foot. Their names, for those hardy souls who insist, are (respectively) *posterior tibialis, flexor digitorum longus* and *flexor hallucis longus.* The last plays a major role in the take-off for jumps or movements of propulsion; it momentarily holds the big toe to the ground and then releases it like an arrow.

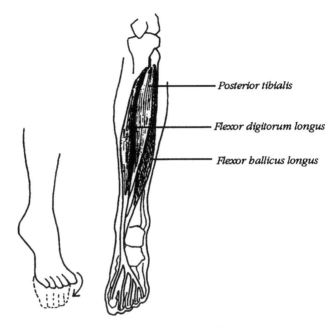

Figure 81. Deep posterior muscles of the lower leg

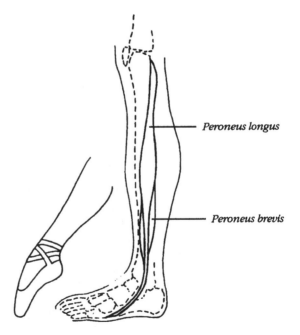

Figure 82. Lateral muscles of the lower leg

The *peroneals*, two muscles that run down the outer side of the calf, also participate in plantar flexion and are the strongest pronators of the foot. They arise at the head of the fibula, adjacent to the insertion of the lateral hamstring. Their tendons pass behind the outer ankle bone, winding around and through the transverse arch of the foot and bracing it, finally attaching themselves to the inside cuboid bone.

The peroneals abduct the ankle; their contraction presses the heel forward and keeps the toes back. A nicely judged balance between the calf muscles and the peroneals produces the correct position of the pointed foot with its maximum stretch along the inner border and into the first three toes. An exaggerated "winged" foot is produced by diminishing the stretch over the ankle and intensifying the contraction of the peroneals—a position sometimes deliberately adopted by dancers to disguise some real or imagined shortcoming, especially in arabesque. A sickled foot, on the other hand, is produced by contracting the muscles that pass along the inner ankle bone, consequently stretching those on the outer side of the ankle. Neither of these two positions is harmful, provided the foot is not weight-bearing; however, the sickled foot is, of course, aesthetically unacceptable.

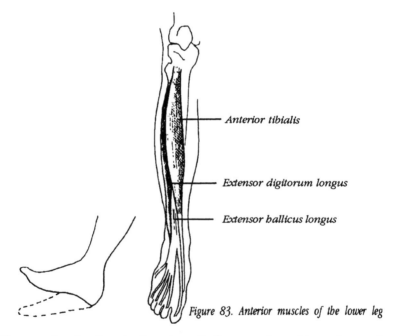

Anterior tibialis

Extensor digitorum longus

Extensor hallicus longus

Figure 83. Anterior muscles of the lower leg

The muscles that flex the foot dorsally (turn up the ankle or the toes) run down the front of the lower leg and pass to the inner side of the foot. For the dancer the most important muscle in this group is the *anterior tibialis*, the tendon of which is readily visible in the front of the lower leg, passing over the ankle joint. From there it travels to the inner cuneiform bone and into the base of the metatarsal of the big toe. This muscle flexes the ankle joint and inverts the foot. When weight-bearing, it plays an important role in maintaining the arch — its twitching and flickering has traditionally signaled proper work in the supporting foot. It is important that the muscle be visibly relaxed during a demi-plié; its contraction will prevent gravity from completing the movement and thus inhibit the plié.

Two underlying muscles in this group turn up the big toe and four small toes respectively; their names are *extensor hallucis longus* and *extensor digitorum longus.*

Last but by no means least, the *intrinsic muscles of the foot* are four layers of short muscles on the sole of the foot; they work together to play a major role in holding the toes firmly along the floor in standing, in propelling the foot in stepping and springing, in maintaining the arch and in controlling the shape of the foot. Their action in completing the curve of the pointed foot, and the many ballet exercises that contribute to their strength, were described on page 102. The origins and insertions of these muscles are confined to the foot itself.

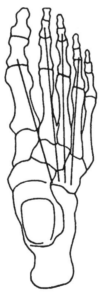

Figure 84. Diagram of the intrinsic muscles of the foot

The alert reader will have noticed that the muscles that turn up the toes are "extensors" and those that point the toes down toward the sole of the foot are "flexors." In other words, in professional language that is the antithesis of our own, anatomists refer to turned-up toes (but not ankles) as being "extended," and pointed toes as being "flexed." Another small mystery is the reference to "the leg" in anatomy texts — it means the lower leg, below the knee. (You may need this information if you find yourself in the position of wanting to look something up in an anatomy textbook.)

There is no doubt that the mechanism of the foot is complex, but when we consider the daily wonders this amazing piece of bodily architecture performs for us, it seems ungracious to begrudge the half-hour or so needed to gain a rudimentary understanding of it. Keep in mind that the muscles that are *contracting* are the ones that move the bones, an anatomical fact which probably runs counter to your kinesthetic sense. It certainly did to mine, when I first encountered the information.

Questions For You To Answer:

Name the two principal arches of the foot.

How many different kinds of movement can take place in the ankle joint?

Where are the muscles that stretch the ankle joint and point the toes?

What are the five tasks undertaken by the intrinsic muscles of the foot?

What are the traditional ballet exercises designed to
strengthen these muscles?

9

What We Say, And What We Mean

It is hardly surprising that outsiders find the jargon of the ballet class-room incomprehensible, but the fact that students themselves often do not really understand their teacher's directions comes as a distinct shock. Yet this is the case—even in some upper-level students. Some-where along the way, they have missed out on a full explanation, if one was ever given. No one ever said teaching was easy; this concern is just one more of the many things a conscientious teacher must remember to address. Here, then, to make matters easier for all, is a rundown of the more commonly used phrases and their meaning.

Don't sit in your plié. The action of plié is one of continuous motion. When the depth of the plié is reached, the upward movement must begin immediately. Any pause at the the depth of movement is referred to as "sitting." In a demi-plié the ascent usually takes the form of a rebound into the next movement. A hesitation at the depth of the descent eliminates this rebound, so that the dancer must re-engage the impetus of the movement. This is sometimes referred to as *using a double plié*. In a grand plié, sitting is often accompanied by a slacken-ing of the abdominals and places a great strain on the knees. It is also contrary to one important purpose of the exercise — to limber and make supple the legs by a continuous flow of movement.

Use your plié. The demi-plié is the mainspring of the dancer's motion. From the potency of its rebound comes the impetus for all types of movement: controlled adage, slow and fast relevés, little bouncy jumps, and different kinds of elevation. Each must be served accurately by the quality of the plié that precedes it—short and sharp, deep and slow, and everything in between. If you are on the receiving end of this correction, you are either sitting in the plié, or using an inappropriate one. Unless you are finishing a movement phrase,

113

always think of the plié as the beginning of the following movement, rather than the completion of a movement just performed.

Center your spine. The reference is to the spinal column—the bodies of the vertebrae stacked one upon the other — and not to those visible knobs running down your back (see page 19). The centering of your spine in plié is basic to your control, especially in allegro combinations. Success in getting centered is largely dependent on the amount of turnout you can obtain in your hips.

Pull up. Frequently given as a catch-all correction for almost any technical difficulty, this must be the most misunderstood directive in our ballet vocabulary. The resulting ugly and harmful distortions cause many of us to wish we could banish the command into limbo forever, but it seems to be with us to stay. If you receive this correction legitimately, you are not resisting gravity sufficiently to perform the movements you are attempting. Your placement probably needs correction; possibly you have flaccid abdominals; almost certainly your spine is too relaxed. In any case, to be pulled up, you mostly need to pull down. An explanation of this apparent paradox begins on page 29.

Don't use your quads. You cannot flex your leg or fully stretch your knee without some contraction of the quadriceps. This instruction means that you are using the quadriceps inefficiently; the leg is probably foreshortened and the balance between the quadriceps and their antagonists, the hamstrings, is out of kilter. Actively engaging the hamstrings encourages the quadriceps to do its work without clenching; a well-placed pelvis, lengthened lumbar spine and a proper turnout in the hips will discourage the quadriceps from overworking (see page 58).

Use your inside muscles. A more positive version of "don't use your quads," but even more vague. In the turned-out position of the leg, the medial hamstrings are the principal inside muscles; their action in flexion of the leg to the front or to the side is one of release, not contraction. *Yet this directive does work.* Imagery is performing its magic here: concentration on the feeling of length down the inner leg reinforces the releasing action of the hamstrings and does away with any tendency to "grip" with the quadriceps.

Pull down your shoulders. Tension transmitted to the muscles that elevate the shoulder girdle, especially the upper trapezius (see page 76), causes them to contract and raise the shoulders. If you are repeatedly given this correction when moving, it is time to pause and figure out what is causing the tension: could it be faulty placement? If the correction is aimed at your posture in general, it pays to be selective about which part of the shoulders you are pulling down, especially if you are raising your arms. Pull down the muscles of your neck and your upper back all along the spine; this action allows the body to work in the way it is designed (see pages 71, 73). Pulling down in the vicinity of the shoulder *joint* is contrary to the mechanics of the joint and provided the muscles in the area, especially the anterior serratus (see pages 74-75), are functioning normally, should not be necessary.

Feel your arms in your back. The discussion on muscles of the upper torso, beginning on page 73, describes the complex role of the muscles of the back in arm movements. However, if you receive this correction the problem is probably a simple one: you are not rotating your upper arm, an action that immediately engages the muscles of the upper back. It is not a good directive, however, as in endeavoring to comply, dancers are apt to pull the shoulder blades toward each other, an action sure to interfere with the freedom in the use of the arms (see pages 71-72). Widen across the upper back from armpit to armpit, and then inwardly rotate your upper arm. Make sure the muscles of your *lower* back are fully engaged.

Lift up out of your hips or **You are sitting on your hips.** Do not raise the front of your rib cage in response to this correction; instead, lengthen your lower back and make sure your abdominals are engaged (see also *Pull up*, on page 114).

Raise your chest. Be careful about this one — a strained high chest and consequent displacement of your rib cage or shortening of your upper back can lead to many problems (see chapter 6). Raise the top of your breastbone slightly without involving the lower ribs. Then widen your shoulders and visualize your neck growing longer.

Don't lift your hip. Usually this instruction means that the hip of your working leg is raised, throwing the body out of alignment. Given that your placement is otherwise in good order, the problem is probably a careless turnout. If you are fully utilizing all the turnout the working leg can command, there will be no lifting of your hip.

Use your feet. The propelling action of the foot is not reaching fully into your toes, probably because of weakness in your intrinsic muscles (see page 111). Any book containing remedial exercises will offer several ways of strengthening these muscles and should be heeded. Over the long haul, however, correct execution of the traditional barre exercises, especially in battements tendus, dégagés and frappés, will exorcise the problem. Check to be sure that you are using your toes strongly against the floor when you are performing these movements. Are the toes of your supporting leg properly accepting their share of the weight in all exercises (see page 27)?

Pull up your ankles. You are probably rolling your feet (placing undue weight on their inner border). To align your ankles correctly (see page 103), first check that you are not forcing your turnout beyond its capability, and then check the placement of your pelvis. Once these important details are in order, spread your toes and use them as an anchor from which to adjust the position of the ankle.

Lift your chin. The alignment of your head is faulty — probably it is forward of center. Whatever the problem, lifting the chin will not correct it. Instead, attend to the root of the trouble—the alignment of the spine. Visualization is the quickest route to success. In your mind's eye, see those vertebrae neatly stacked especially in the upper thoracic and cervical areas (see Chapter 3). "Hang by your head from a star," advises Mabel E. Todd in *The Thinking Body.* Make use of some of the imagery on page 29 and devise some of your own.

Get up on your leg. You are "sinking" onto your supporting hip, allowing it to drop and to move outward from the midline of your body. You need to galvanize all the muscles of your trunk on the side in question and make sure you have a well-pulled-up supporting ankle. If you are still in trouble, you probably have weak abductor muscles (see pages 46, 47, 48).

When In Doubt, Ask

It is surprising how reluctant most dancers are to question their teacher —partly, I believe, because interrupting the class is unthinkable, and by the time the last port de bras has been completed, the question has flown out the window. But try to remember it, for mind and body are one: fog in the head translates into vapor in the limbs—so ask, and ask again.

10

Conclusion

A dancer's knowledge of the body in motion is profound. There is not a great deal in these pages that the accomplished professional dancer will not have figured out by trial and error or come to know by instinct. But trial and error could have been largely eliminated and instinct reinforced by a practical understanding of the science at the service of the craft.

As dancers and teachers of dance, we have inherited a tried and tested technique, which, like that of any art form, is constantly evolving. The innovations in contemporary choreography gradually come to be reflected in the daily classroom; the traditional vocabulary is built upon and expanded. We do not dance in the manner of our predecessors of fifty years ago.

But while artists lead the way, as always, it is the movement scientists who have quickened the pace of this evolution in recent years, largely because of the new information they are making available to us. Our task as dancers is to keep our minds open and receptive to these new insights, and to evaluate their relevance in the light of our own special knowledge of ballet technique. That knowledge had better be sound; otherwise we can too easily become victims of the many hazy and inaccurate "scientific" theories that circulate from time to time in ballet studios all over the world. These conceits are invariably based on partial truths propounded by charismatic teachers; many a promising career has faltered as a consequence.

I hope these writings will provide our emerging dancers and teachers, when faced with conflicting pronouncements, with the additional tools they need to make their own decisions, decisions based on real scientific evidence and on their own experience of movement, rather than on the latest fad or half-digested fact. I would also like to think the information will give the more experienced among us the ability to articulate *in scientific terms*, when necessary or appropriate, the principles we know to be truths.

117

Endnotes

1. Good sources of information on injuries, remedial exercises, etc:

   L.M. Vincent, M.D. THE DANCER'S BOOK OF HEALTH, Kansas City, Andrews & McMeel, 1978.

   Sally Sevey Fitt, DANCE KINESIOLOGY, New York, Schirmer Books, 1988.

   Raoul Gelabert, ANATOMY FOR THE DANCER, 2 volumes, New York, Dance Magazine, 1964.

   Andrea Watkins and Priscilla Clarkson, DANCING LONGER, DANCING STRONGER, Pennington, New Jersey, Princeton Book Company, 1990.

   Dr. William Hamilton, DANCE MAGAZINE, February 1978–January 1979, January 1983, April 1983, April 1984, May 1984, July 1984.

2. L.M. Vincent, THE DANCER'S BOOK OF HEALTH.

3. Image given by Dr. Lulu Sweigard in HUMAN MOVEMENT POTENTIAL, New York, Harper and Row, 1974.

4. Image from Dr. Werner Platzer, in COLOR ATLAS AND TEXTBOOK OF HUMAN ANATOMY, LOCOMOTOR SYSTEM, Chicago and London, Year Book Medical Publishers, 1978.

5. Rhonda Ryman of the University of Waterloo, writing in DANCE IN CANADA, No. 16, Summer 1978.

6. An article by Terry Trucco on Cynthia Gregory, DANCE MAGAZINE, June 1991.

7. Image given by Irene Dowd in a lecture to students in her New York studio.

8. V. Kostrovitskaya and A. Pisarev, SCHOOL OF CLASSICAL DANCE, Moscow, Progress Publishers, 1979.

9. Sparger: 60 degrees to the front, 40 degrees to the side, 15 degrees to the back; Vincent: 65 degrees to the front, 45 degrees to the side, 15 degrees to the back.
Note: Since many reputable kinesiologists report much less pure hip movement, we may assume that the figures given above apply to the turned-out leg.

10. Rhonda Ryman and Donald A. Ranney, in a paper presented at the ADG/-CORD Dance Conference, Hawaii, August 1970.

12. Dr. William Hamilton, DANCE MAGAZINE, April 1978.

13. W. Hardaker, L. Erickson and M. Myers in THE DANCER AS ATHLETE, ed. C.G. Shell, Champaign, Illinois, Human Kinetics Publishers, 1990.

14. Dr. Platzer's book is intended mainly for medical students but is easy to read, beautifully illustrated, and perfectly comprehensible to the layman. His information invariably confirms the basic tenets of classical ballet technique, and has been the source of much of the material in *Inside Ballet Technique*.

15. Marilyn Klaus, teaching in her New York studio.

16. Hamilton, Vincent, Gelabert, Watkins and Clarkson, et. al.

17. Dr. Lulu Sweigard, HUMAN MOVEMENT POTENTIAL.

18. Janice Barringer and Sarah Schlesinger, THE POINTE BOOK: SHOES, TRAINING AND TECHNIQUE, Pennington, New Jersey, Princeton Book Company, 1990.

19. Dr. William Hamilton, DANCE MAGAZINE, February 1978.

20. Teachers in the U.S. can obtain these free brochures by calling 1-800-234-4858. Overseas teachers can write: Capezio/Ballet Makers Inc., 1 Campus Drive, Totowa, New Jersey, 07512, U.S.A.

Bibliography

Works Cited in the Text

Merrill Ashley. DANCING FOR BALANCHINE. New York, E.P. Dutton, 1984.

Janice Barringer and Sarah Schlesinger. THE POINTE BOOK: SHOES, TRAINING AND TECHNIQUE. Pennington, New Jersey, Princeton Book Company, 1990.

Sally Sevey Fitt. DANCE KINESIOLOGY. New York, Schirmer Books, 1988

Henry Gray. GRAY'S ANATOMY, Philadelphia, Running Press, 1974.

Tamara Karsavina. CLASSICAL BALLET: THE FLOW OF MOVEMENT. London, Adam and Charles Black, 1962.

V. Kostrovitskaya and A. Pisarev, SCHOOL OF CLASSICAL DANCE, Moscow, Progress Publishers, 1979.

Werner Platzer. COLOR ATLAS AND TEXTBOOK OF HUMAN ANATOMY, LOCOMOTOR SYSTEM. Chicago and London. Year Book Medical Publishers, 1978.

Karel Shook. ELEMENTS OF CLASSCIAL BALLET TECHNIQUE. New York, Dance Horizons, 1977.

Celia Sparger. ANATOMY AND BALLET. London, Adam and Charles Black, 1949.

Lulu E. Sweigard. HUMAN MOVEMENT POTENTIAL. New York, Harper and Row, 1974.

Mabel E. Todd. THE THINKING BODY. New York, Dance Horizons, 1968. THE HIDDEN YOU. New York, Dance Horizons, 1976.

Andrea Watkins and Priscilla Clarkson. DANCING LONGER, DANCING STRONGER. Pennington, New Jersey, Princeton Book Company, 1990.

A. Vaganova. BASIC PRINCIPLES OF CLASSIC BALLET. New York, Kamin Dance Publishers, 1969.

L.M. Vincent. THE DANCER'S BOOK OF HEALTH, Kansas City, Andrews & McMeel, 1978.

Related Works

Although not directly quoted in the text, the following books have been the author's source of inspiration, insights and companionship during the writing of this book.

Rose-Marie Laane. DANSE CLASSIQUE ET MECHANISMES CORPORELS, Paris, Editions Amphora, n.d.

Anna Paskevska. BOTH SIDES OF THE MIRROR: THE SCIENCE AND THE ART OF BALLET. Pennington, New Jersey, Princeton Book Company, 1981, Second Edition, 1993.

Gretchen Warren. CLASSICAL BALLET TECHNIQUE, Tampa, Florida, University of South Florida Press. 1989

Ann Woolliams. BALLET STUDIO, New York, Mereweather Press, 1978.

Index